YOU CAN'T LEARN IMPROV FROM A BOOK

Alan Hawkins

SEATTLE, WASHINGTON

Alan Hawkins
Seattle, Washington
www.alanhawkinsimprov.com

You Can't Learn Improv from a Book / Alan Hawkins. -- 1st ed.

Front Cover Photography
James Murphy
trainmanphotography.com

Back Cover Photography
Bill Grinnell Photos

To my family:
My wife Amanda and my daughters Amelie and Sawyer.
I would be lost without you.

To my best friend:
John Masier, I love you brother.
Thank you for always being there for me.

CONTENTS

SPECIAL THANKS

The teachers and directors that showed me much of what I wrote in this book:

Janice Noga
Brian Roberts
Susan Kehler
Randall Stump
Nancy Miller
Elizabeth Fiester
Dan Pessano

My improv teachers (partial list)
Amy Seeley
Tom Booker
Scot Robinson
Joshua Funk
David Razowsky
Craig Cackowsky
Marc Evan Jackson
Matt Elwell
Rich and Rebecca Sohn
Susan Messing
Mick Napier

And the entire crew at Unexpected Productions.

IN LOVING MEMORY

Lynda Hawkins, my mom. Thank you for always believing in me. I could not get to the place I am without the rocket engine of support you provided. I miss you dearly.

Randy Stump. The strong hand shoving me forward, as I stumble through my life, will always be yours my friend. You took a gearhead and made him into an Actor. A Stage Manager and a Director. You could see my strengths often when I could not. You were the one who first hired me to teach your high school students. This book only exists now because of you.

Kevin Guzowski. You jerk. You left us when things were just getting interesting. I miss you anytime I am on stage. Because you should be there with me. I miss talking smack with you and meeting up for dinner. The beer and burgers were good, but the company was most excellent.

Jay Leggett. What a soul you were. I learned so much about directing improv and sketch from you. Many of the ideas in this book were inspired by notes you gave. I will always treasure listening to you hold court at The Hollywood Improv. Sitting at the end of the bar like a king as comedy legends were casually walking around. Sitting there with the rest of my friends, as you told us stories of Chicago and the many movies and TV shows you were on. Bless you for the wisdom of comedy that you gave so freely.

PRAISE

Alan is an absolute gem of an improv teacher. He not only understands how improv works, but he can articulate his brilliant ideas to a wide range of students—from high schoolers to old timers, like myself. He is less concerned with just "entertaining" an audience than he is in crafting dynamic, engaging scenes and characters, which of course leads to much more entertaining and thoughtful theater! In five short weeks, he took our improv team from absolute novices to professional improv-ers, and radically changed how we approach our improv preparation and performance!

-- **Josh Butchart**

In his pursuit of comedy, Alan Hawkins has honed himself into an improvisational gadget/weapon/tool that is as sharp as it is playful, a weapon that empathizes even as it cuts deeply, scything away bad habits and shallow flim-flam with surgical precision. Ignore him at your peril. He has helped lift many an improviser and team into a higher level of performance and I am grateful to call him my friend, mentor and compatriot.

-- **Matt Larsen**

It has been my great pleasure to know Alan Hawkins and watch him perform. As someone who is known as an ambassador in the global improv scene, I can confidently say that there are very, very few who share Alan's level of passion and commitment to the preservation and dissemination of this great art form and what it has meant to my life and so many people who have brought me joy over the decades. Space run, do not space walk to your suggested location and buy this book!

--Brain James O'Connell aka BOC

Alan Hawkins is the rare bird of improv: He's a great teacher AND a wonderful improviser. He not only understands how improv works

best, but he can also clearly and concisely pass that elusive information onto the improv student.
--David Razowsky

Alan Hawkins is an improv guru. What sets Alan apart from other improv teachers is his ability to assess your best qualities and amplify what you are already good at. He breaks you of your insecure habits, too...and he does it without crushing your spirit. He's been trained by the old guard of improv and he knows how to be gentle with the sensitive new kids. Alan is the best!
--Anna Miller

Alan is a seasoned performer, a study of human behavior and an incredible acting coach. He is able to create trust almost immediately and encourages each performer to focus on relationships on stage, above all else. Alan listens deeply and provides constructive feedback that is useful and motivating. His notes are insightful, full of compassion and succinct enough to be remembered and added to any improviser's toolkit. What I love most about Alan is how much he cares: about people, about the art of improv and about helping others. He is a remarkable coach and gifted improvisor.
--Jonni Ressler

Alan's incredible talent, stage presence, humor, and easily understood methodology enable him to bring out the best in each of his students. His kind feedback, combined with a supportive and fun curriculum, fosters success and laughter. His step-by-step guidance is both logical and empowering. I left his workshop more confident and at ease in my skills than when I walked in. I use his techniques regularly when I perform. Alan is brilliant!! Buy this book!!
--Taylor Dahlia Edwards

FORWARD

When Alan asked me to write a forward for this book, obviously I was both honored and excited by the opportunity. But when faced with the daunting task of putting my thoughts into the written word, I was quickly reminded of why I started improvising to begin with. So here we go....

Having dedicated over two decades to being a public-school teacher and an improv instructor in the greater Chicagoland area, my extensive experience has brought to light an obvious pattern among educators. It is not uncommon for us to feel apprehensive about teaching content that we ourselves may not feel we have mastered. However, since improvisation is about taking risks and going with your gut, I invite you to do just that.

As the director of The Second City's Youth/Teen Ensemble from 2006 to 2020, I had the extraordinary opportunity to collaborate with countless motivated and talented teens. They were not only eager to learn improvisation and the process of creating their own original revue, but also enthusiastic about sharing their voices, perspectives, and outlooks on life. For these high schoolers, improv served as a platform to comment on the world around them, take creative risks, discover their true identities, and celebrate their successes. The immediate gratification they experienced came from knowing that their ideas were not only received but also processed and enjoyed by individuals of all ages. I have witnessed firsthand the transformative impact of improv on young minds.

You Can't Learn Improv from a Book is a guidebook of creativity and exploration. In this insightful manual, you will embark on the exciting adventure of teaching improvisation to high school students. Improv isn't just about laughter and quick thinking; it's a powerful tool for fostering teamwork, boosting confidence, and unlocking the untapped potential within each student. This book, written by Alan, my close friend and former director, provides a roadmap for both novice and experienced teachers, offering practical exercises, valuable insights, and a wealth of anecdotes that illuminate the profound benefits of incorporating improv into the high school drama curriculum.

Get ready to watch your students not only embrace the spontaneity of the moment but also develop crucial life skills such as communication, adaptability, and creative problem-solving. The chapters ahead serve as a compass, guiding you through the dynamics of teaching improv and offering a toolbox of ideas to make each lesson engaging and memorable.

Improv isn't just an art form; it's a mindset. As you delve into the pages that follow, I invite you to embrace the joy of discovery, to celebrate the unexpected, and to witness the remarkable transformation that unfolds when students are empowered to express themselves freely and fearlessly. Remember, this book serves as a guide for you. The exercises are all completely malleable. Veer off course, make discoveries, create new opportunities stemming from the years of knowledge and experience Alan is sharing with you.

I invite you to allow this book to support you on the exciting journey of teaching improv to high school students, sparking not only laughter but also a lifelong love for self-expression and collaboration. Here's to discovering the limitless potential within every student, and yourself!

–Jessica Rogers

SPECIAL NOTE

It takes a special person and a special talent to be able to be an improv director or coach for high school teams. Same with being a good improv teacher for high schoolers. Not everyone can do it. Back when I was producing the "Teen Comedy Fest," Alan Hawkins was one of our improv teachers we chose year after year to teach at TCF. Alan always got great reviews from the students and their teachers too. Alan has the special ability to be able to remember what it's like being a teen and teen doing improv as beginners or with years of experience. He always led his TCF workshops with clarity, empathy, intelligence, boundaries, creativity, focus, and fun. Because of those skills his TCF students experienced what he instructed and had a great time playing together in a structured environment.

Now that I've told you how experienced and how good Alan is, let me tell you about his book. Let's say you're a high school teacher, director, or coach, and your communication or drama kids want to try improv. How do you start? Where do you begin? What are the best steps and best practices to take? Well, the great news is that you have it all in this book. Alan's book is essential for anyone who wants to start or continue an improv class or show for any high school groups. Everything you need is right here. From getting started, to running classes to rehearsals, from getting ready for a show to running a show. Everything is written with a strong point of view that guides the reader into success. The concepts and vocabulary of improv games and techniques he writes about are crystal clear, with the intentions, purposes, descriptions, all easily laid out and show how to do everything and why to do it. By covering a nice wide range of games, scenes, and longer formats, there's plenty in here to keep any high school class, workshop, or team happily occupied for years to come.

The great thing about Alan's book is that it's applicable for high school groups, college groups, or really any or all improv groups just getting started. So pick it up, buy it, read it, and let Alan guide you on how to start playing and doing improv. You'll be glad you did.

– Jonathan Pitts

ABOUT THIS BOOK

I created this book originally for drama teachers who choose to teach improv to their students, but have little to no experience with it. This book is all of the exercises and games I use in my workshops, laid out as a step-by-step lesson plan that builds to an ultimate goal. You can teach the lessons in this book as a complete lesson plan, or break it into 2, 3 or 4 levels of study. I also go through how to use these games and lessons to put up a short form (games) improv show, or a longform improv show; including presentation, show dress and how to host a show.

HOW YOU CAN USE THIS BOOK

The lessons are laid out with the help of other drama teachers that I have worked with over the years. Each section includes:

Title (self-explanatory)

Game/Exercise

Each game or exercise builds a specific skill and each build on the previous one.

Director's assist

I intend this to be the thought I would give if you asked for advice on how to run these. These are notes to help you know what to look for. These are not for your players.

How the game is set

How the players set up for the game / exercise on and off stage.

Number of players

Group means all the players you have. The rest is self-explanatory.

The stage

There are not a lot of set pieces on an improv stage. I typically have four chairs onstage.

How to play

I will explain how each exercise or game can be played.

Notes for players

Feel free to discuss what they mean to you and what they mean to the group. Improv is best learned through doing it, watching it, talking about it, and last through reading about it. Hence the cool name of the book.

Terms in this book

- **Warm-ups –** Warm ups are fun repetitive exercises meant to relax our minds, stretch our bodies and get us into a mode of being playful. They should be done as a group before improvising.
- **Game –** A game can be performed in a show. All games have a lesson in them.
- **Exercise –** An exercise is something that builds a mental muscle and adds skills to a player's tool belt that is not something you would do in a show.
- **Backline –** This is a line of players standing upstage. Players step out of the backline and perform exercises / scenes / games and then step back.
- **A line up –** This is an exercise/scene /game where the players perform in a line downstage.
- **FREEZE! –** The host or the director can yell this to pause a scene or the game.
- **SCENE! -** The host or the director can yell this to end a scene or game.
- **Circle up! –** Most warmups are performed in a circle. I usually will yell this out when I want to start rehearsal.

These exercises are set in order to work up to doing improvised Shakespeare scenes. But you can also do them in any order you wish. All are good exercises on their own.

Dressing for Rehearsals

Ideally you want your players to dress comfortably to do a lot of movement and rolling around on the floor etc. Same as a rehearsal for a play. Flat bottom tennis shoes and comfortable attire Tell them to dress like they are going to learn a dance or to workout.

The stage

You don't need to have an actual stage, but I do recommend you set up the class with seats facing a play area with a wall at the back. You can set up chairs in a semicircle for the audience. I recommend placing at least two chairs on the stage for players to use.

A few words about teaching and directing improv

If you are new to improv or new to directing improv, I have a few tips that will be helpful.

Scenes or games or whatever people do on stage and call improv should be about relationships. Relationships are the glue that holds this whole deal together. It's not about being funny. It's about being relatable. My good friend and teacher Tom Booker gives the great note "Scenes are about relationships, and they should come from a place of love." I share this because he is telling us we do not have to be in love in our scenes, but we should at least like each other and want to spend time together. If I were to present you with two doors, behind Door #1 is a lovely house party, where people are chatting and enjoying each other's company on a sunny day. Behind Door #2 is the same group of people, but they are all arguing and telling each other what to do. "Outside it's raining, in the distance you hear thunder..." which room are you drawn to? Which one would you want an audience who paid for tickets to go into?

Establishing a relationship in a scene

There are a few easy paths to establishing a relationship in a scene. However, defining them is often difficult when you first try. The first thing a player needs to get past is the fear of being funny. A player that is worried about that will start with the wildest, out of left field statement like "I'M A HALF DOG HALF CAT PERSON! MEEE-WOOF!". That's someone who is worried about all the things. The better path is to look your partner in the eye and say how you feel about them. This is applicable through the whole scene. At any time, if a player feels lost in a scene or game, just look at the other player and make an honest statement about how you feel about your partners. Another way to establish a relationship is to physically / mentally mirror the other player. Once we align with each other we have a strong relationship because we are both the same person.

Everything that is true about directing a play, is true about directing improv.

This is theater. Actors should show up on time.

Actors should cheat out and find their light. The audience should be able to see your face.

The stage is a safe place. We should not feel like we are in danger on stage. Respect boundaries. You should respect your actors and they should respect each other.

Acting is a journey. Your directing should be the light that helps players find their path. Look at where they are struggling and come up with games and exercises that will help. I look at each exercise or game as a tool in your tool belt. I will explain what tool each of the exercises in this book are and do for a player. In time you can expand with your own.

Use negative notes sparingly. A positive note will be taken, but a negative note could end up ringing through the ages. Choose your battles wisely and figure out how to constructively guide your player to the place you are trying to direct them.

Live in the moment, don't think and amazing things can happen. There is no beginning, there is no end, there is only right now.

- Brent Tubbs

Everything you need is in your scene partners face. Stop trying to do something. Look at your partner and say how you feel about them. Anything else is a distraction.

-David Razowsky

Whatever your scene partner says on stage is exactly what you needed to hear. And hearing it is a relief.

-Susan Messing

1

WARMUPS

Warming up before improvising is a vital part of the art form for a few reasons:

1. Improvising a shared activity that is simple and not scene-based gets everyone on the same page.
2. It helps the players relax their minds from the day-to-day noise we all experience.
3. It helps everyone get into a mindset of play and playing together.

When we are kids, playing comes easy. It's natural for a child to explore and play. As we grow older, we judge ourselves. We worry about being judged by others. All of this noise in our heads makes it difficult to just jump into improv.

Warming up will help everyone get into game-mode. Explain these ideas to your players:

1. Make eye contact during warmups. This will help everyone be connected.
2. Your goal should always be to make the other person look good. If they have the same goal, then both players will look good.
3. Relax. Have fun. Play.

These are also good notes for improv in general.

All of these are done with the players in a circle. As the director, you should warm up with your players. You need to be relaxed and in a state of play as well.

Here are my favorite warm-ups that I have encountered in all parts of the world:

Tell Me About Your Day.

Have everyone pair up. What we want to do is get everyone used to just talking to each other. Have all of your pairs find a space away from everyone else. Explain that you want them to just describe their morning to each other. They should talk to each other honestly, asking questions about what they hear from the other person. Let this go for around three minutes. Walk around the space and listen in on bits of the conversations. When you're ready, yell "FREEZE!" Now, note that what they did is very much what improv is all about.

They made a statement about the suggestion ("What did you have for breakfast?").

They listened to their partner and responded to the last thing that was said.

They probably did not make a joke.

That is it. At the heart of what we are attempting to do is Listen, respond honestly, and repeat. That, at its heart, is what we are trying to do. Recognize when someone said something honest that got a reaction.

Counting

This is a listening warm up. The group drops their heads and closes their eyes. The goal is to count as high as you can without talking over each other; if two people speak at the same time, you start over at 1. Tell your players you will always start. Say "One," someone else will say "Two," and so on and so forth. Tell everyone to relax and let others have their space. It's also just fun to see players want to win the challenge. Encourage the fun. Laugh.

Zip-Zap-Zop

Looking across from you, clap but let one hand travel forward to clearly point at another player and say "ZIP!"

They will then do the same motion to someone else, but they will say "ZOP!" Pointing at a new player.

That player will then, with the same motion, clap and point to someone else and say "ZAP!"

This will repeat across the circle until everyone gets really good at it. That's your cue to start a new warm up. We want to keep them on their toes.

Pass the clap

Look at the person next to you and put your hands up like you are about to clap. The other player will do the same. Clap in unison. Then that player will look to the person next to them and repeat. Move in a clockwise fashion.

Remember, you want to make the other player look good. They want to make you look good.

Once the clap has successfully gone around the circle a few times you can say "Ok, let's speed it up! Continue to make good eye contact." When everyone is going pretty good with that you can introduce some variations:

1. Someone receives the clap, but instead of passing it onward, they pass it back to the person who passed it to them. (Clap. Then making eye contact, Clap back.) Now the clap is going back the other way.
2. Clapping across the circle: If you receive the clap, make eye contact with someone across from you and pass the clap to that person.

Now the clap can travel both directions around the circle as well as across it.

Word ball

This is a word association warm up. Looking across the circle, say a word to someone across from you. Something simple is best.

"Kitten"

Whatever word that makes them think of, they will then say a new word to someone else across from them.

"Cute" the next person might say something like "Baby" or "Dress."

It doesn't really matter. It's only important that people listen to the last thing that was said and respond honestly to that.

GO

This is done across the circle. Pick someone to start. If you are warming up with your players, you start. Here's what you will do:

Look across from you at a player and make eye contact. Say "Go."

They are going to walk toward you to take your place. You need somewhere to go. Find someone else and make eye contact with them. When they say "Go," start walking to take their place. And so on and so forth.

Some things to remember: We want to make each other look good. Don't rush to take someone's place. If they said "Go," you start walking. If they haven't gotten a "Go" from another player you should slow your roll. Give them time to get a "Go" and move to make room for you.

Eye contact, listening, and agreement are all at play here. It's not a speed-walking competition.

Zero x1 x2 x3

For this warmup you will need enough room for all of your players to move about freely.

First explain that everyone will be walking around the room. Everyone has a forcefield around them that prevents them from touching anyone else. You want them to focus on themselves yet navigate the space. It's also a good idea to let them know where they can't go. They need an arena.

On a safety note. Let them also know this exercise never includes running.

Zero – Ask your players to casually walk around the space without taking the same path twice in a row. Focus on themselves. Let this happen for a little while until you feel they are all comfortable. Explain that this is level Zero.

x1 – Now tell them "Let's speed up to a Level One." You can let them know that they will go all the way to Level Three, so one should be faster than zero, but not super-fast.

x2 – Now tell them to take it up to Level Two, still being mindful of not bumping into each other or whatever is in your space.

x3 – This should be mall walking speed.

Now that they are familiar with how this works you can have them change from a Level Three down to a Level One into a Level Zero. Change the speeds as you see fit. I would just suggest getting them back to level Zero to relax them.

2

OPENING LINES

What this game teaches us

The most common worry in new players is not knowing what to say at the beginning of a scene. This is an exercise designed especially to show how easy it is. You also want to show your players that they do not have to put a great amount of effort into being funny. Funny is most often a side effect of being honest. If you think about it, most of the time someone tries to be funny, the opposite happens. This exercise is also a great way to accept the suggestion and put your own unique spin on it.

Director's assist

Have your players form a line facing you. I like to tell everyone "Don't worry about being funny. Be honest and the funny will happen." Advise your players to keep their lines simple since they will be repeating the line a lot. To introduce this first exercise ask the group "Who is worried they won't know what to say at the beginning of a scene or game?" Most likely, all of them will raise their hands. Great! (I always raise my hand as well.) Explain that this warm up will help with that. I really love this exercise because it is a simple method to get new improvisers using the suggestion through making a statement and supporting their partner by making a character choice and defining a point of view at the beginning of a scene.

Example

The suggestion is "Kittens." An example you could give would be something short like "Kittens are cute and fluffy." It doesn't matter as long as it is true to them.

Number of players

Group

The stage

Form a backline facing forward.

How to play

Once they each have their own statement, tell them that they will be repeating it in different styles. I like to start with "the Old West" and that style is whatever the Old West means to them. Hopefully you'll hear an old prospector saying, "I don't like kittens" or a gun fighter saying, "Kittens are cute and fluffy."

Once everyone has said their line in that style, keep it up by giving them more styles.

My favorites are -

- Soap Opera
- Shakespeare
- Action Hero
- A very old person
- Flirtatious
- Angry / Sad

By the time you have done half of these, everyone is laughing. Here's what's noteworthy: These lines all had a great foundation for a scene. They started with an honest statement inspired by the suggestion. They had a strong character choice. The players were being honest with their own opinion of the suggestion. This should be the first exercise you do each time you get together. In time, everyone will be able to just do it from you yelling out suggestions. They will come up with a short, honest statement and then add a random character or emotion. Once players get really good with this exercise, they can start multiple scenes in minutes, and all of them will have a smart, strong opening.

Players' assist

Even if you do not know how to do the style that is suggested, just do your best. Not everyone can do a lot of accents and characters. If you don't know what to do, mirror some of the other people. If you're up first, confidently go with your gut.

Eventually you will want to get them to where they can just come up with their own likes and characters over and over based on one suggestion.

Now let's move onto some short scenes.

3

THREE LINE SCENES

What this game teaches us

This game shows us how to be more expressive in our scenes, which then has the benefit to better inform ourselves and our partners. We can also surprise ourselves and the audience by saying more about what we are improvising. Instead of saying "I'd like a soda..." what if they said "Yes, I would enjoy a Pineapple Fresca!" Suddenly, we're hanging out with a person that prefers Pineapple Fresca!

Director's assist

This exercise is great for two reasons:

1. It's funny as all get out to hear people talk like this. Because no one does that.

2. If the suggestion is "Hat" I would rather hear a player say "You, madam, have a beautiful hat atop of your head" than "You have a nice hat..." What you're shooting for as director is players who have lines once in a while that's between the first example and the second. When we get to Shakespeare, we will want them to hit the last example on the head. HARD. (But, let's keep that between us for now.) Now rotate those players to the back and repeat until they all have done it. If it's going well, switch the side that gets to say the first line and run it again. This is a great way to get players warmed up and saying beautiful things.

How the game is set

Split the group into two lines facing each other. One side will have an opening statement. If they don't know what to say, advise them to start their line with "I" or "You," that way we don't get random noise like "The sun is bright today..." remember, scenes are about relationships.

Number of players

Group

The stage

Bare stage

How to play

Tell them to keep their lines short and to remember what they said because they are going to do the same scene three times in a row.

An example would be –

Player 1 – You have a nice hat.

Player 2 – Thank you! My mother gave it to me.

Player 1 – You have a great mom!

That's it. Short scene. Short lines. Now, ask them to do it again, but to use MORE words and more expressive words WITHOUT adding any new information.

Player 1 – You, madam, have a beautiful hat atop of your head.

Player 2 – My most profound thank you my good man! My own mother gifted it to me.

Player 1 – You my friend, have a most amazing mother!

Can you see the difference? I like my villains to be overly verbose, in improv it's essential. Now have these players do it once more, but ask them to add as many words as they possibly can WITHOUT adding any new information.

Player 1 – Dearest madam, I only aim to burden you with great news! It is my opinion that the accoutrement atop of your head is the most marvelous hat that I have ever seen in my life!

Player 2 – Dear sir, please accept my most profound and sincere gratitude! My own birth mother bequeathed it to me.

Player 1 – The matriarch of your family is a real hero and her greatness is legendary!

That is it. Have those players rotate to the back and do the next pair.

Once everyone has gotten the hang of that, keeping the same format let's start working with a new exercise that builds off of the last one. These exercises and games should build on each other. Note that it's easier to respond when someone has a more well-formed idea.

4

STEAL A LINE

What this game teaches us

This exercise is the best use of "Yes, and..." without saying those words and is something used again later in this book. It is great for avoiding new/invented lines that do not have anything to do with the scene. If you steal lines from your partners, you stay on topic, talking about each other and not things or people outside of the scene.

Director's assist

Remember, scenes are about relationships. Always tell your players that. It's much better to say what you really feel about the other person than to try to make up something funny. Trying to be funny in improv is usually when things fall apart. Tell your players to be honest, funny will take care of itself.

How the game is set

It is the same as Three Line Scenes. Split the group into two lines facing each other. One side will have an opening statement.

Number of players

Group

The stage

Bare stage

How to play

Stand in two lines that face each other. One line will be the opening line. (The opening line is always a statement. No questions.) Players will start their first lines with an "I" or "You."

Player 1: I love the hat you have on.

The next person needs to use a part of that statement in their response.

Player 2: Thanks, mom! I have this hat on to protect my skin from the sun.

The first player also needs to use a part of the other person's line in their response.

Player 1: Yes, Terrance, You do need to protect your skin from the sun, you are a redhead after all.

SCENE!

Those players now move to the end of their lines. Once everyone has cycled through, do the exercise one more time, the second line will begin this round.

Some notes to give to help your players

This is an exercise that is useful for listening and heightening an idea. Tell them to get into the habit of responding ONLY to the last thing that was said. They can also take something the wrong way: take a compliment as an insult or an insult as a compliment. Improv is about being surprised. Why not try to surprise yourself first?

5

CORE EXERCISE: THE SUGGESTION

There is an agreement in improv, and it's very important to a show being successful. It goes like this:

Come to our show, and your ideas will be used to create instant theater.

That's it. That's what an improv show is. You show up. Give us something we didn't think of and we will make your idea into something entertaining. But what often happens (like, a lot of times) is a suggestion is given and then nothing is done with it. The audience feels cheated a bit. The players didn't keep up their end of the bargain. The best way to do this is to make a smart statement about the suggestion in the first line. The way I go about this takes a bit of work, but I'll guide you through it with some exercises.

Once I hear the suggestion, "Spaghetti," I immediately go through what I know about "Spaghetti." My first thoughts are pretty simple:

Spaghetti = Food. Messy. Italian. Inexpensive. Dinner.

Ok, I can come up with a first line of dialogue with any of those. But let's go a bit deeper.

Spaghetti = Romantic dinner. Dinner a parent can make fast and cheap. Dinner that can come in a variety of sauces and extras like meatballs, garlic bread and salad. But the place I really want to go is the next level.

Spaghetti = Was originally from Asian cuisine brought to Italy via the trader routes. Sometimes the only food my kid will eat. My mom made a lot of spaghetti as a single parent because it's super cheap and easy.

So, now I have a lot of information to start my scene. If I have the first line I would check in with what my partner is doing, how they're standing, what's our dynamic? Then make my first line something like "Mom, I made spaghetti dinner so you wouldn't have to. Sit back and relax..."

Or, let's say I look at my partner and they seem to have a stern look to them. Maybe I can get a little intellectual. "Spaghetti is just another stolen idea. One culture stealing noodles from another and packaged up on the cheap to keep the working class malnourished and meek!"

The scene for either of these won't end up being about spaghetti. Instead, they will end up being exactly what we want in improv: They will be scenes inspired by the suggestion. By making a smart, informed choice at the beginning of the scene, you have a fully informed character to start off with. And all of those other ideas I listed? Those shouldn't ever go away. If you're improvising a game or a longform set, those ideas can pop up again later. You should carry the knowledge of the suggestion in the back of your mind at all times during the show.

WIRE ACT

What this exercise teaches us

How to physically manifest what status our character is.

Director's assist

This exercise is from Viewpoints, an acting exercise that David Razowsky adapted to improv. I recommend making this an exercise you do with your players as much as possible. The whole idea here is to give your players the ability to physically embody a character with little effort. If two players are up and the suggestion is "Prince Phillip in a can" and player one looks at player two and says "My Liege! I have your can of Tuna!" player two can rise to high status by imagining a wire at the top of their head. Immediately they will have the posture of someone who is high status. They will know how that person sounds. How they walk. If you can teach your players this skill successfully, you will have some interesting scenes.

Number of players

Group

The stage

Bare stage

How to play

Give your players as much room as the space allows. If there is a place off limits to them wandering into, like a light booth, tell them.

Some notes to give to help your players

Tell them to relax, listen to their bodies, notice their movements, and to be affected by how others are moving.

Wire Act

In this exercise you will need to have enough space for all of the players to move around freely. Just like the movement exercise x1 x2 x3 have everyone move about the space at a zero level. You are going to explain that each of them will have an imaginary wire that is attached to a part of their body. This wire is pulling on that part. Let's start at the top.

Head

"You have a wire attached to the top of your head! It's pulling up. This means you will walk like a member of royalty. A king, a queen, your status is set to HIGH!" Explain that they should still have their feet flat, but their spines are straight, shoulders back. Now, as they are walking, ask them to make nonsense sounds in the manner this person would speak, careful not to use actual words. They can say "Blah-blah-blah", but it should sound like how this person would sound, whatever high status means to them.

Shoulders

Shift the wire to the shoulders. This is not a king. This is a soldier, a manager of things, the head is not held as high, but they are not a low status. They can sit at the same table as a person of high status but will never be that. How does this person sound (still no words)? How does this wire change their walking pattern? Since they are not being pulled up by the top of their heads, they can have a more relaxed gait. Maybe their arms move a bit more freely.

Chest

The wire is now attached to the chest, but instead of pulling up its slightly (we are not looking for ape-like movement) pulling them down. This person is now low status. They work hard at life. Their spine is a bit more bent; they might have a more shambling walk. What sounds would this person make when they talk?

The next level of this exercise is to have everyone form a circle. Ask one player to enter and tell them where the wire is pulling on them from (head/shoulders/chest). Have them vocalize as that character (no words, just nonsense sounds). Now have a second person enter the circle (if no one volunteers, just pick someone) give that person a wire and once you feel they have the movement down, have them vocalize.

They can be the same or different. You can have two kings, two queens, a king and a low status person and so on and so on. Once you feel they have their roles down tell them to talk to each other. Just a few lines. Doesn't matter what. We just want to hear them talk to each other from their point of view. When they have done three- or four-lines yell "SCENE!" and ask them to rejoin the circle. Have a new player enter and do it again. Let everyone have a few chances.

Eventually they will have this down and you can instruct them to enter and pick their own status. Just first tell them to make eye contact, look at how each player is being pulled and recognize that status. At this point they don't need to make noises; they can just start small simple scenes.

7

TIMES 10

What this exercise teaches us

This game shows players that they can heighten their own ideas and characters. It *is* possible to “yes, and...” yourself.

Director’s assist

You’re trying to get them to take ideas and characters a step further from the get-go. By pushing their characters way past where they would ever imagine taking them on their own, they can see the means to do it to about 50% of the highest point.

How the game is set

You’ll need two players; have one plug their ears. while that one can’t hear as well, get the suggestion of a generic character like a cowpoke or a British school teacher. Now, have the other player plug their ears and get a similar suggestion for that player. I suggest someone with an accent. Now have the two players take a seat. Tell them they are at a café. Remind them –

Is the scene about the café? No.

Is the scene about what they are eating? No.

What’s the scene about? The relationship.

Number of players

Two

The stage

Set up two chairs like a café table.

How to play

In this exercise you will need two players and a bell. First do this exercise with them seated. Give each player a type of speech or an accent (please, no disability or stutter. Be respectful). A New York accent and a French accent both are always fun to play. Tell them you want them to talk to each other about what they had for breakfast, but in their suggested accents. Instruct your players to start small with these accents. Now, tell them that every time they hear a ding from the bell, their accent is going to get ten times bigger. Which means, if my math is correct...

Ding! X10 Ding! 10x10 Ding! 10x10x10 and so on. Within about five dings they should sound like blabbering fools, which is what you want. Everyone is going to laugh.

Some notes to give to help your players

What sounded the best? After the first or second ding? Or the last? What you will find is that everyone agrees that the last bell was hilarious, but after the first and second dings, they were sounding a little cool. If everyone is in agreement with this, ask them if they ever felt lost in a scene? Or they wished their character choice had a bit more flair? Well, now they can ding the bell in their own heads. Nothing is stopping them from applying that bell to a funny walk or a hand gesture. They can heighten their own deal just by thinking "I'm going to ring the bell a few times in this scene..." and see what happens.

8

CELEBRITY TAXICAB

What this game teaches us

That we can always mirror our scene partners. Especially if we do not understand what they are doing.

Director's assist

Tell your players that they should only aim to copy the person who gets into the cab. You are not looking for two perfect Lady Gagas only that they mirror the other person.

How the game is set

Two chairs side by side with a little space in between. Like a car. Have a person sit in the driver seat, they are neutral until the first rider comes in. One the passenger side, have everyone form a line to get into the car.

Number of players

Group

The stage

Two Chairs

How to play

We're going to play a game you might know called Taxi. You need two chairs set down stage center. That's the car. It's got a driver's seat and a passenger seat. Have all of your players line up on the passenger seat side just behind where the back of the car would be. Whomever is first in line should sit in the driver's seat. Now, explain that they will be getting into the taxi as a celebrity. It does NOT have to be a good celebrity impression! They just need to be some sort of celebrity. They will wave to the cabbie and then get in and start talking as their celebrity. The person driving needs to imitate them. So, if the person is doing an Elvis impersonation. The driver will also become Elvis and we will have two Elvi (I think that's what you call multiple Elvises?) or two Lady Gagas or two Christopher Walkens.

These two will have a short scene, then the one driving will find a reason to exit the vehicle and go to the back of the line. The person left goes to neutral and moves over to the driver's seat to pick up the next celebrity. And so on and so on, until we get to the original driver and they initiate as a celebrity. This is another game from my good friend Amy Seeley. She teaches sketch writing and character creation courses online and is simply brilliant (see link in resources section).

Some notes to give to help your players

Here's what you are looking for from this exercise: When the players imitate these celebrities, they probably have a strong point of view from the get go. Reiterate that to them and ask if that made it easy to keep in character. Ask them how it was to see two Elvi in a car talking about being Elvis. It was probably pretty funny. Note that no one had to make a joke during this, they only needed to have a point of view and be honest. Also note that if they have ever done a scene and someone started with a character or an action and they did not know how to react, it's a very strong move in improv to just mirror them. Even if you don't understand what they are doing, you will be supporting their choice and the audience will at the very least find it interesting. More likely than not, they will find it funny.

EMOTIONAL STAGE

What this game teaches us

This game shows us that we can change emotions. And, having emotions in a scene can ground us and connect us to our scene partners

Director's assist

Explain to your players that they should find reasons to move to different parts of the stage (This is a great habit to have in improv) They can go to the same or opposite orbit each other but also find times to be on the same level

How the game is set

This game is traditionally just two players. They will perform a scene based on a suggestion. Start with asking for a relationship they might have.

Number of players

2 players

The stage

Place two chairs.

How to play

In this game, the stage is split vertically into five sections. Each section represents an emotion as the players stand in it.

Far stage left is Joyous.

Stage right of center is Happy.

Center Stage is neutral. No emotion. (This is like a reset.)

Stage right of center is sad.

Far stage right is angry.

Notes for players

Move around! Try not to spend too much time with the same emotion. Listen to your partner, how does what they are saying affect your character? Don't just show us the emotion, let us know how that emotion is changing your point of view.

CONDUCTED EMOTION

What this game teaches us

Like Emotional Stage, this game shows us that we can change emotions. Having emotions in a scene can ground us and connect us to our scene partners

Director's assist

Explain to your players that they will both be experiencing the same emotions at the same time unlike Emotional Stage where they will have the choice of different emotions. This will be an example of mirroring each other. Mirroring is a strong move in any scene because it is the ultimate "Yes, and.." of your partner.

How the game is set

This game is traditionally just two players. They will perform a scene based on a suggestion. Start with asking for a relationship they might have. You will need a volunteer to be the conductor. Explain to this person that they will be the conductor by saying each emotion they feel is necessary or not necessary.

Number of players

2 players

The stage

Place two chairs.

How to play

The conductor will call out these emotions. The players on stage need to show us how that emotion changes what their own character is feeling about the other.

The conductor can call out -

Joyous.

Happy.

Neutral. No emotion. (This is like a reset.)

Sad.

Angry.

A good suggestion is to ask them to let the players experience each emotion for a bit, the conductor is a participant in creating a good scene. They should want to make the players on stage look good. Now in a live show, the audience volunteer will not be held to such a standard. And that is part of the fun.

Notes for players

Same as Emotional Stage, listen to your partner, how does what they are saying affect your character? Don't just show us the emotion, let us know how that emotion is changing your point of view.

Stop. Collaborate and listen.

-Vanilla Ice

A good relationship is a competition of generosity.

-Madonna

Listening is all there is.

-Kevin Guzowski

11

GROUP SCENES AND GAMES

As you do improv, you will notice that people can more easily find a relationship in a two-person scene, but much like life, when you add more and more people the relationship(s) get... complicated. And a lot of them fall into a gang-mentality where one person ends up being the bad guy/person who messed everything up/is doing "it" wrong. This happens because it is safe. It is so much easier to have an argument scene than a real scene with people who like each other because you are afraid. Luckily the improv gods were smart enough to create games that encourage players to work together in group scenes. I have a few exercises to mix in as well.

PRODUCT PITCH

What this game teaches us

This game shows us how to listen and respond only to the last thing that was said. It also shows how being silly and accepting the craziest idea as the best idea, creates enjoyable theater that the audience likes.

Director's assist

This is another game where you want your players to surprise themselves with what they can come up with. If the suggestion is something like "SPAM: Now with Bluetooth 5.0!" we want our players to not only accept that this crazy idea is a good one, but we also want to see them make it even crazier!

Comedy is the art of hanging pretty pictures in a house that is on fire. The only way to make a multiple person scene work is if we all agree on what's going on NOW. Not about things that happened in the past, or what might happen in the future. What is happening RIGHT NOW? You want your players to do that. Just what's happening on stage. In a rehearsal type setting begin with the counting warm up before playing this game. Tell your players you want them to think about the others taking space on stage, and to listen for them to be done so that we can yes, and. . . their ideas. It's all about making the other person look good.

Since my goal is to make you look good, and your goal is to make me look good, we are all going to end up looking good.

How the game is set

Set up four chairs and tell your players that this is a corporate board room

Number of players

Four+

The stage

Four chairs, possibly a table if you have one handy.

How to play

Someone will get the suggestion of a product name that does not exist. Like Tofu Tires! Or Cat Umbrellas! Your players now need to come up with these things in the scene:

- Name of the product
- Slogan for the product
- Target Audience that will love the product
- And where to sell the product

If the suggestion is Bluetooth SPAM meat product. Then it might go something like:

Player 1 – We will call it The SPAMTOOTH 5000!

Player 2 – I love it! And our slogan will be "Stay in touch with your lunch!"

Player 3 – That is an amazing idea! And the target audience will be busy Moms on the go!

Player 4 – You are blowing my mind! And we will sell it at crafts stores because that where Moms like to go!

SCENE!

Some notes to give to help your players

Encourage them to compliment the person that spoke before; not only does that mean they need to listen; they also have to respond to the last thing said. All multiple person scenes should go like this: respond in a positive way to the last thing that was said. My friend and teacher Susan Messing once told us in a class "The last thing you heard, was EXACTLY what you needed to hear. Good or bad, hearing it is a relief." Tell that to your players.

CORE EXERCISE: ENTRANCES & EXITS

Entrances and Exits is a great group scene teaching tool. Tell your players that they can only exit if they first say why they are leaving when they hear their assigned word. "I made brownies! I'll go get them!" When that person leaves the rest need to talk about them. This does two things: it informs your partner about themselves and it informs you on how you feel about them.

Now let's do a variant on this game that I created

ONLY TWO REMAIN

What this game teaches us

It teaches us that it's ok to leave a scene. You need to announce what you want when entering a scene so your partners can know your intentions.

Director's assist

Tell your players that these are short scenes. They can be independent of each other, or they can be a continuation.

How the game is set

Two people start onstage. Get a location that will fit on the stage, let's say a gym, because that's the first suggestion you will get. Everyone thinks about the gym, even if they never go.

Number of players

Group

The stage

Set two chairs just anywhere. Players can use them or not. Their choice.

How to play

Start with two players. Have everyone line up on one side, the rules are this:

There can only be two people onstage at one time. When someone enters, one person needs to leave.

The person leaving must say why they are leaving.

Someone needs to say something about the person who just left.

This does not need to be sequential but can be. We want to follow the story of the most interesting character or idea.

Players can return as often as they like.

Some notes to give to help your players

Have a good feeling about the other people on stage, show us why they like each other. Like Product Pitch, they need to take what they hear and show us how it affects them.

CORE EXERCISE: MONOLOGUES/POETRY

This is exactly what it says. Set up an audience section where you and everyone can sit facing a stage area (it's fine if you don't have a stage, just set up an area). With this exercise, I highly suggest you start so that they can see what is expected of them. Stand center/down-center stage and explain that you are going to tell a short story about something that happened to you in the last 24 hours.

Explain that you are not looking for them to be funny or dramatic. You just want an honest short story about a part of their day. Relax your shoulders. Take a deep breath and just start talking in a conversational tone. "Today I got up and made my favorite breakfast, an everything bagel from Einstein Brothers Bakery. I love their bagels, just the right amount of chew to them without being like a piece of cake. And they never put too many toppings. I toasted it just enough to get a golden brown on the inside halves and then used their low-fat whipped cream cheese. I had a cup of coffee and some grapes and it was just wonderful."

The end.

That is it. I mean, make up your own, that's my breakfast story. You're just showing them that all they have to do is talk for about a minute. No need to make jokes. No need to be funny. Just an honest short story. Ask everyone to do it just once. You want players to get into the idea of planting themselves center stage and talking.

Director's assist

Stand in the back and tell them YOU need to hear them clearly. This is theatre, they should project to the person in the back of the room so everyone can hear them. If they do something short, that's fine. We want the action of this exercise rather than its duration. If someone has the gift of the gab, and just goes on and on, go ahead and call "SCENE!" at a minute or two, they obviously got it.

POINT OF VIEW

What this exercise teaches us

How to give our characters more depth on the fly.

Director's assist

This exercise is intended to give everyone the knowledge that they have everything they need in a scene or a game.

How the game is set

Players form a backline and each will step forward to speak.

Number of players

Group

The stage

Bare stage

How to play

You want to hear the player's honest opinion about a subject. Have a player take the stage and ask them "What are you an expert on?" You are looking for something they love; it could be Star Wars, it could be building miniature sailing ships in a bottle. It doesn't matter. Then when they have it, ask them to explain why it's better than X? So, why is Star Wars better than Star Trek? Why do they love dirt bikes rather than 4x4 trucks? Same as above, this does not have to be long. Just an honest one- or two-minute monologue.

Now, the second half of this is the real fun. They are going to have to act like they are an expert on a subject that does not exist. Like: please explain why horses love to be ridden. Or, tell us why Abraham Lincoln was actually a great baseball player.

Director's assist

Explain that they want to use the same mental muscles they did when they were talking about something they already knew a lot about, but in this case, they are making up all of the facts on the fly. You know... improvising! Overall, they will have an instant point of view about the suggestion, even if they know nothing about the history of popcorn production in Russia in the 1980s. If this works well try one more time, but now add a wire from the wire exercise. Make them high status, and ask them to explain how much people in high society enjoy eating Jello.

Suggestion + point of view + status = Instant and honest characters.

Some notes to give to help your players

Be honest to your character. Find that truth that they need to fuel them for the time that character is onstage.

A PATCHWORK OF MONOLOGUES

What this game teaches us

Like the counting game this teaches players to listen and find their own space to take over the monologue.

Director's assist

This is basically Conducted Story, except that everyone is playing the same person and giving a first-person type of narrative. Players can be told to run this sequentially or in order, but everyone should get a chance to do it. If you are doing it in order, you can call out the last person in line to end the story.

Number of players

Group

The stage

Bare

How to play

One person is at centerstage. Give them the suggestion of a line of dialogue that is optimistic like "Today I finally learned…" or "I knew it would happen someday!" The player onstage starts their monologue with that line. They can be a character or themselves. If they are an obvious character, then everyone needs to mirror that character as best they can. When someone wants to take over, they walk to center and tap the person talking. The person talking will continue until they feel that tap, then even if they are mid word, they stop, and the next player needs to finish that half-unsaid word.

POETRY SLAM

What this game teaches us

To be thematic in our improv. To say more beautiful things in our scenes.

Director's assist

These are not poems that need to rhyme; instead, they are more thematic.

How the game is set

Players line up downstage center.

Number of players

Four to five

The stage

Bare stage

How to play

This sounds harder than it actually is. First, know this: No one has to rhyme anything. It's great if they can, but a poem doesn't have to rhyme. What it does need to do is paint a picture with words. And that's what I want you to tell your players. You're going to do two different kinds of poems – a beat poem that includes the idea of "The Great Lie" and a love poem.

Let's start with the beat poem. Have five players form a backline. Explain to them that they are going to improvise a poem about a great lie that has happened to the AMERICAN people. Now this isn't conspiracy theory stuff, because your suggestion to start us off for them will be something like "Christmas presents" or "Breakfast cereal." Tell your players that they will use the suggestion of "Breakfast cereal" to create a beat poem that exposes the lie of breakfast cereal.

Explain that they first need to find a hook, like a song. The reason is that a poem and a song are very close. One just has a backing band. A hook is any thematic phrase that is said at the beginning of a verse. Listen to almost any Beatles song and you will hear the hook.

They want to find a simple thematic phrase. You are going to give everyone the same suggestion. Let's go with "Breakfast cereal." My example of a hook for that would be:

Toasty Os oh Toasty Os! Toasted rings of LIES!

OK, well... This ship is ready to sail. Now you need to expand: Why are they rings of lies?

Toasty Os oh Toasty Os! Toasted rings of LIES!

Your colorful box promised me a nutritious and healthy start to my day!

But your hollow flavor left me with nothing but an empty pit in my belly.

I even doubt that you have even seen the inside of a toaster! Your rings... Taste stale

Toasty Os oh Toasty Os! Toasted rings of LIES!

The colorful hippo on your box, with its toothy grin, with so many teeth? I think not. Oh! You advertise whole grain goodness with essential vitamins and nutrients. But I think you have more in common with the box you arrived in, than a balanced breakfast!

Toasty Os oh Toasty Os! Toasted rings of LIES!

Toasty Os oh Toasty Os! Toasted rings of LIES!

Toasty Os oh Toasty Os! Toasted rings of LIES!

This is my riff on a poem. Feel free to use it in your class, but you can see where I'm going here. Be thematic. Use the facts you know about cereal and be presentational. Rhyming is a very small part of this exercise. If someone can, that's great. But do not sweat it.

Let them all do this and do a short poem.

Now, have them do a love poem. This is the same idea. You want a hook that anchors what you are doing. You noticed that I repeated the last line three times, that's literally because I didn't know how to end it. So I just repeated my hook a few times because it sounds artistic. If your players don't know what to say, but they have a hook, just say the hook over and over until they find the next line.

For the love poem, you need to fall madly in love with the suggestion. Let's say the suggestion is "First car."

I remember the first time I saw Buggy. It was the first time I truly felt... Freedom. Buggy was a 2001 VW Beetle. Buggy was yellow with a black racing stripe someone had placed on the hood. Sure, Buggy had some dents and was missing a hubcap.

But with Buggy, it was the first time I truly felt... Freedom!

Buggy wouldn't always start on cold days. Buggy only got one station and the cassette player worked, but... Who has cassettes?

But with Buggy, it was the first time I truly felt... That I was free!

Buggy wasn't the fastest, or the coolest. But, Buggy was mine!

One day as I was parked at Cheddar's Burgers, I was inside with my friends. I don't think that trucker saw my poor-poor Buggy, but we all heard the CRASH inside Cheddar's.

Buggy... Left me that day. Without my Buggy in my life... It was the first time I truly felt... Lost.

snapping

Now I know what you are thinking "My players aren't going to do that!" I bet if you give them the chance they will and it's going to be funny and surprising. As for what this does for improv, it lets us be more thematic in our play. What if players every once in a while, said a line that was like a quote from a book, or said something to a loved one that sounded like a love song? That would make for a powerful scene.

CORE EXERCISE: OBJECT WORK & MOVEMENT

What is object work and why do we do it?

Object work is done to build the set and create the props to perform scenes. It finds its roots in Mime and Theatre Del' Arte. But it is really neither of those things. I'm very good at object work and movement but would never call myself a Mime. I have not done the work and study to earn that distinction. I recognize that improv owes a great debt to the work those artists have done. The exercises I offer are specifically "Object Work," not Mime. I make that distinction out of great respect.

Object work is essential to good improv. It paints a fuller picture of your scenes, informs us about ourselves, and lets the other players have fun along with us. But the players need to always be mindful of what others are doing. Especially if you are taking into account that the audience is always watching. If you set something down on a table that isn't there, and another player didn't see that? Odds are that player is going to walk right through that table.

Object work informs us about who we are. If I sit down and use object work to show I am holding a cup of tea, the way I hold that cup, the way I am drinking from it, the way I react to having that moment, all combine to tell me who this person is. And if the other players are watching, it may inform them as well. What ways can I show that I'm drinking tea instead of coffee? I could be dunking the tea bag or extending my pinky and daintily sipping my brew. It all informs you and your scene partners. If you know Mime, or clowning exercises, introduce them when doing this section. It's highly valuable to performing good improv.

Giving objects weight and space

There are a few objects that are always present when a player is just starting off in improv: A drink, a phone or a pistol. And they are almost always done in this fashion:

The drink – The player forms their hand into the shape of a letter C and then presses their closed mouth to their thumb and tips the hand up like they are somehow taking in fluids in this fashion.

The phone – The player forms their hand in the Hawaiian symbol called Shaka and then places their thumb into their ear and their pinky near their mouth and will then proceed to speak into their pinky.

The pistol – The player forms a finger gun. And whatever happens next just goes downhill from there.

If we had an actual cup or glass in our scene, would you still hold it in your hand in the shape of the letter C? And then, take it a step further and put your lips to your thumb instead of the rim of the drinking vessel? No. And a phone? Unless I'm at work, I don't even answer my phone. And if I did, it's not even shaped like a handset. It's a slap of glass and aluminum that I rarely hold to my head. But let's say I did. While holding it, my thumb is not in my ear. I'm not even going to go into having a gun in a scene. We should avoid that at all costs.

But I digress.

Here are some exercises that I suggest you first do on your own, then teach to your players. Real object to pantomime – Take a broom. Walk to a space in your house and start to sweep like you normally would then stop. Let's check all of this out.

How are you standing? How are your feet? Are they parallel to your shoulders? Look at your hands. Is the handle of your broom thick or thin? Are your hands close together on the handle or further apart? There is no way that your hands are in a fist because the broom takes up space in your hands. If it's not there? Your hands should still be open like it is. Get it? Great!

Start sweeping for about 30 seconds.

Stop. Are they sweeping away from you? Towards you? Side to side like a psychopath?

What kind of sweeper are you?

Ok, put the broom aside. Relax your body for a moment and now let's sweep without the broom. Reach for your imaginary broom. Grab it, remember the weight and the size of it. Remember how you stand when you sweep. Start sweeping like you normally do.

Congratulations! You're doing good object work!

We need to show our audience that our imagined props and sets have space and weight associated with them. This is how we convey that. Now go get a coffee cup and fill it with a chosen beverage. Water, Gin, whatever. I'm not going to judge you. Take that to your table and have a seat. Take a deep breath and relax your body for a moment. Let's pick a time of day for this. Let's go with morning. This is your chosen beverage for the morning. Reach out and pick it up.

Stop.

Let's look at how you did that. Did you grab the handle? How did you grab it? Three fingers and your thumb? All your fingers and your thumb? How do you normally hold a cup? Look at how your arm is, your elbow.

Now, let's take a drink.

Did you sip? Did you take a good gulp like I do my coffee? What is your other hand doing? How heavy is it? Is it a big mug that you got from the farmers market, thick and formed with a fancy earthen glaze? Or did it come from Disneyland and say something like "Don't mess with me until I have had my coffee and churro." Do it once more, noting all of this and put it aside. Now do all of those things exactly as you did with the cup. Imagine if you did that in an improv scene; do you think everyone would have a good idea of what you were doing? I bet they would.

Here's my next task for you. Go around your kitchen and open and close the cabinet doors, the fridge, turn on the faucet. But watch how you are doing it. Now, step away and find an open space and recreate those actions in pantomime. Build your imaginary kitchen in an empty space. If that works and feels good, step back and take it to the next level. You have built your imaginary kitchen, let's use it. Make a sandwich.

You have everything you need. Show us what each item is as you use it. You are sharing your object work so we can all know what you are up to and possibly to play with it ourselves. If you feel like you have it, now you can use this same method with your players. They do not have to be in a real kitchen. Explain to them all of the things I explained to you and ask them to find a space away from everyone else.

Have them sweep. Check them out and assist as you can. "Hey, your hands are close up, give your broom space." Have them stop and check in with themselves. Then let them sweep again.

Have them sit and drink. Then, have them imagine their own kitchen and make themselves lunch. From here on out, no finger phones or drinking from their thumbs.

How object work informs our characters

Have you ever looked at how someone eats? How do they hold their sub sandwich? How do they hold a doughnut? Have you ever noticed the way someone does something and think "That's so them?" That's how our object work can inform who we are and inform our scene partners.

Now we want to play a little game of assumptions. Two players take the stage. One is going to be doing an action, like eating a doughnut or knitting. You're going to give them a little secret. If you like you can write it down on a piece of paper.

You are eating the first doughnut you have ever had and it is INCREDIBLE!

Or

You are knitting angrily. You are not angry at your scene partner. You are just angry as you knit a blanket. The person who is doing the object work is mute. They need to show us who they are through their actions. The other person needs to verbalize all of their assumptions about them in the form of statements that start with either "I" or "You."

"You really hate knitting..."

"I think you are a person that loves doughnuts."

These do not have to be long scenes. Just three or four observations and then switch out one player. Have the player that is left do the action this time or vice versa. You want to give everyone a chance to perform each role.

Director's assist

We want to show how we can interpret in our minds what someone's object work means to us. Even our own. This is an exercise that will build those muscles in our scenes. Noticing how a person is standing can tell us about how they see their own status, how they love or hate, it's all there if we take the time to look and even if we don't say it out loud, we can say in our minds "They really have a thing for pasta..." and that will give us the room to say "I like pasta too... I like this person. We have things in common."

PARALLEL PARKING

What this game teaches us

We can set stage pictures by deciding to move in a certain way.

Director's assist

Just like Entrances and Exits, players can justify why they are standing or moving in a certain way.

How the game is set

This game can be set with two or three players. No chairs.

Number of players

Two or three

The stage

Bare stage

How to play

Ask your players to wander around the stage. At some point yell FREEZE! Now tell your players to check in and notice how far apart they are from each other. Now they need to always be this far apart no matter who moves, and they should find reasons to keep moving.

Some notes to give to help your players

Tell them to have fun with being pulled and pushed as others move. This is a great game for a shortform show. And a great game to do in the style of Shakespeare.

21

SIT, STAND, LEAN

What this game teaches us

Just like Parallel Parking, we can always be playing a game like this in our scenes. Especially if the scene becomes just a few players standing around talking. Scenes are more interesting when people move.

Director's assist

Explain to your players that they should keep changing to the different positions. Also, to avoid getting into the trap of a three-person scene, which is two people picking on the third. If you notice this a lot, you can add an emotional layer to the game.

The person sitting is always sad.

The person standing is always happy.

The person leaning is always neutral.

Number of players

Three players

The stage

One chair center stage. Players can move it if they want.

How to play

In this game, just like the title suggests, one player should always be sitting, one should always be standing, and one should always be leaning. If someone is not, the audience can call them out by quietly saying "uuuuuuuummmm..." While this is happening, they will do a scene based on a suggestion of a location or a relationship. Or they could even be building something together.

Some notes to give to help your players

No one is anyone's boss or manager in this or any multiple person scenes. They all have the same status. We do this so that we don't get caught up in a teaching scene. No one wants to watch a teaching scene. Trust me.

Don’t tell us what we already know. Move forward, not back.

-Jay Leggitt

Be honest to what’s happening on stage. Be honest to your character.
Be honest in the moment.

-Randal Stump

Scenes are about relationships. Relationships are about love.

-Tom Booker

YOU MOVE, I MOVE

What this exercise teaches us

We should always be affected by our partner. We can mirror their movements, or we can do the opposite. This is a great exercise to get players out of just standing and talking.

Director's assist

This is a mirroring game. Imagine a player as a pendulum. Each time they swing away from their scene partner, the other is affected. First have them do the opposite movement, then have them copy the movement.

How the game is set

Players form a loose circle. Give the players enough space.

Number of players

Group

The stage

Bare Stage

How to play

No one can speak until you give them permission. Ask one player to step into the circle and walk around at a casual pace. Then ask them to start exaggerating some movement they are making. Then ask them (within the safety of their own body) to exaggerate the movement once more. Now, ask someone to join them and either mirror them, or do the opposite of them. Once you establish a good groove, ask someone to make a statement, just whatever this arrangement is making them feel like. The other person should respond ONLY to what was just said. Let the scene go for four or five lines and then call SCENE! Ask a new person to enter the circle and repeat. Do this until everyone has had a chance.

Some notes to give to help your players

Explain that once they find their movement, they should look at it through the wire exercise. What status are they? Is the other player mirroring them? Does that make them the same status? Are they doing the opposite? Does that make them lower or higher to them? How does that influence their opening line?

CORE EXERCISE: FREEZE TAG

Hey! Why is Freeze Tag mixed in with object work and movement?!

I'm so glad you asked! (Of course, you didn't. I just think people might.) Freeze tag is another universal game that almost everyone knows. If you don't, here's a quick rundown: The players form a back-line facing the audience. Two players step forward. The host or one of the players gets a suggestion. Let's say "tree house." Those first two players will then do a short scene in that location. At any time (Hopefully, after both players get to have a little scene.) someone on the backline yells "FREEZE!" and the two players freeze in place.

The player that yelled freeze taps one player out and assumes the exact same position and then makes a statement that starts a brand-new scene. And so on, and so on. You probably have played it and probably have had your students play it. I'm going to let you in on a little secret. Freeze Tag is a movement and object work game. If you have ever seen a game of freeze tag and it just doesn't seem to be working, look at the backline. They are looking for a position or an object to assume so they can call out "Freeze!" but the two people are just standing there. On top of that, they are in the same positions that the last scene was in. No one is moving! No one has anything in their hands. Freeze Tag doesn't work without those vital ingredients. So, here is an exercise that will help you. And it comes directly from one of my greatest teachers and dear friend Amy Seeley in Los Angeles, California.

DANGER TAG!

What this game teaches us

Freeze Tag is a movement and object work game. This game teaches players that they should always be on the move while improvising, in Freeze Tag — they should be grabbing objects, moving around the stage, etc. The goal in any Freeze Tag type game is not to do long scenes, but short fast scenes that build quickly and are all different from each other.

Director's assist

This game is like training wheels for any freeze game.

How the game is set

Players form a backline.

Number of players

Group

The stage

Bare stage

How to play

This game works with the same set up as Freeze Tag. But, instead of yelling "Freeze!" a player will yell "Danger!" When the two players in the current scene hear that, they don't freeze. Instead, they assume a new totally unexpected position! The person who yelled "Danger" taps one player out and assumes the exact position the player was in and uses that to inspire the new scene. Etc. etc.

This is a great way to get players to see how freeze tag is a movement and object work game. Make note of that to them. Here are some more tips to make both games work.

1. The player who yelled freeze just walks up, taps a player, assumes their position and makes a statement, inspired by the scene they see. Don't hem-n-haw, don't drag it out deciding which you like better. Let's keep the game rolling.

2. It's a great idea in these games to always be moving, always be holding an object.

3. Make BIG statements! This scene will probably only live for five lines. Why not make those lines huge? "I HAVE ALWAYS LOVED YOU!" It also gives your partner something to respond to.

4. Let your scenes come from a place of love and understanding. Freeze tag is fast and frantic, and we often go negative in those moments. I challenge your players to find moments of happiness and joy instead of negativity.

5. Freeze Tag and Danger Tag are great ways to warm up.

Some notes to give to help your players

Make big "I" or "You" statements in each little scene. Say how you feel about the other player at the top of the scene and see if you caN find a way to show us a change in them.

GOOD IMPROV IDEAS FOR PLAYERS

When I first started teaching improv at high schools, one of my teachers asked me for a list of ideas for students to help them do good improv, ideally one that could be printed on a single page. I failed at that, but I did come up with these that he loved. I have since given it to almost all of my teachers and they have reported that they pass it out year after year to their students. I invite you to do the same.

The only way to fail at improv is to not try.

Funny is a side effect of being honest and smart. BE YOURSELF! 100% of the time a player tries to be funny it flops. Jokes never work. Funny happens in improv because someone has made the choice to be honest and smart. Make statements about what is happening RIGHT NOW.

Improv is about relationships.

In improv there are no strangers. No matter if someone starts a scene with "Hi person I have never seen before! My name is blah-blah..." Have a feeling about that person. Have you ever met someone, and you felt an instant chemistry? Try to have that with whomever you are playing with. The audience wants to see people who like each other. No one wants to see a show where people are mad at each other and yelling. Even if your partner starts arguing it's a good idea to show why you are friends or could be friends.

Make your scene partner(s) look good.

Make this your goal. Your scene partners make it their goal. You will both end up looking great!

There are no mistakes. Mistakes are gifts.

Improv is the world you create with your friends. There is no way to fail if you are at least trying and if something "goes wrong" it's probably the first real thing that has happened. Keep doing it. Make more mistakes.

Start a game or a scene with a statement inspired by the suggestion.

It sounds easy. It makes perfect sense but seems to only happen half the time or less. When a scene starts, look at your partner and say the first thing that comes to your mind (hopefully it's inspired in part by the suggestion). Open your mouth and start talking. Make a HUGE statement at the start of a scene and I promise you and your scene partner will have a lot to work with.

Listen to the last thing that was said. Respond ONLY to that.

Everything your scene partners say is the MOST important thing you ever heard. And it is EXACTLY what you needed to hear.

Change things up. Do the unexpected.

Lost in a scene? Don't know what's going on? Look for something that you can misinterpret. Take a compliment as an insult. Take an insult as a compliment. Do the opposite of what you would normally do. Whatever happens in the first part of a scene or game is what the whole scene or game is about. Don't second-guess yourself or your partner. If you get lost, think about what happened in the beginning of your scene, say or do that again. Even if it makes no sense, do that. You will support your partners and support the suggestion.

Having a character is GREAT! Just have a point of view.

A funny walk or a wacky accent is nothing without something real to back it up. Think of your character as a car. Having a point of view is the engine that drives that car. A point of view will also help you keep that character and if need be, bring it back in other scenes.

Don't let go of your deal!

George W. Bush never stopped being himself and that's what gave comedy writers YEARS of comic gold. BUT! If he ever stopped mis-pronouncing words or saying inappropriate things to the queen of England and said, "I'm just kidding, I'm actually very smart," no one would find it funny anymore. Stick to your deal. If you start a scene as a French person don't let it go. Even if a scene partner says "Sally, you were born in Toledo. You're not French" STAY FRENCH! Dear GOD! STAY FRENCH!!!

Don't fix ANYTHING!

If you are in a scene or game and think to yourself "Oh jeez, this is not (funny/good/whatever)" don't fix it! Break it more! PLEASE don't be a fixer because you think something is not right. It sticks out like a sore thumb, and it tells the audience you don't trust your fellow players. When you think you need to fix something, change your mind and figure out how you can break it more. You will have a better time and your partner will feel your support.

Have an emotion.

(Hopefully a happy one, but sad works. Angry is harder.) Scene not going anywhere? You're both stuck arguing about the tire you are changing and nothing is happening? Look your partner RIGHT in the eye and say how you TRULY feel about them. I bet it will be the first funny thing that has happened. I know I would laugh if a tire changing scene became a wonderful romantic romp. Or a moment of true reflection on what you mean to each other. Much better than one person telling the other that they are doing something wrong...

Be an expert on the suggestion.

If the suggestion you get is "Spaghetti"? Start thinking of all the facts you know about Italian food, who invented it, who loves it, what is it made of? Make a list in your mind. Why? If you have ever been in a scene and didn't know what to say, saying a random fact about the suggestion can get things going again. "Spaghetti is made of flour. I have a wheat allergy..." Is the suggestion "Buddhism" and you are not an expert? Make up a lie and tell it like it's the honest truth. "Abraham Lincoln was a practicing Buddhist." I bet it will get a laugh and jump start a stale scene. Plus, it brings back the original suggestion front and center. Win/Win.

Make eye contact.

Check in with your scene partner. How are they standing? What status do you think they are to you? Look at their eyes. Are these the eyes of a happy person? A sad person? How does that make you feel? Having that moment can help you build an instant relationship.

Move around!

Don't be that person that stands and talks. Imagine that you need to move every time your scene partner moves! It will make a scene more dynamic. If your partner is not moving, orbit them! Get them moving. Two people standing and talking is boring. Let's not be boring in improv.

CORE EXERCISE: MULTIPLE PLAYER SCENES

One thing no one talks about a lot is making a three-person scene work. Almost always, they turn into two people picking on one. And, as a show idea? That does not sound too enjoyable. Here's how to create good three person scenes.

Give your players these notes:

The reason I started with the note about two people going against one is that it is the most common way a three-person scene goes. If you find yourself in a situation where you are the person that the other two are ganging up on, actually say "Hey! Stop ganging up on me!" If you are one of the two and you realize it, change your allegiance to the other person's point of view. By seeing someone else's side of the story you can defuse that negative energy. When you're in a three-person scene, everything your partners say is exactly what you needed to hear at that moment. Good or bad, it's a relief that they said it.

If you're in a three-person scene, and you feel like you are not contributing anything? LEAVE the scene! Make an exit and say why you are leaving "Guys, I gotta go make blintzes! PEACE!" and leave.

If you are in a three-person scene, and someone says "Guys, I gotta go make blintzes! PEACE!" you have a job. And the job is called "That player just left; we need to talk about them!"

"Jeez, Jerry makes a lot of blintzes!"

"Yeah, it's that new fad diet..."

"Oh yeah, the Blintz diet..."

That way, if and when Jerry Returns, he has a few things to go on. Jerry is on a diet. Jerry is eating a lot of blintzes.

Set up three players to do a scene. Give them a suggestion. Now, before they start, tell them everything that is said is THE BEST thing they have ever heard. See how that goes. Then, after everyone has done it, do it again, but add on the layer of asking someone at some point in the scene to exit. Ask them to say a statement as to why they are leaving. Ask the remaining players to remark on that player's exit. Let them know that the player that exits can return with good cause. Another note about people who exit: When you exit a scene in a show, BIG things are happening to your character while they are off stage. Don't let your character become boring just because you left the stage.

Listening – It's all about the Listening.

Listening is a vital skill in improv. When we say listen, it is a higher sense of the word. It's about hearing the subtext of everything that's being said, hearing the emotions of a person and being affected by them. Listening in improv is about cataloging what's being said and being affected by what's not being said. But how do you teach this skill? That's a very attractive question!

SUBTEXT INTERPRETER

What this game teaches us

This game shows us that we need to listen with more than our ears. What is your scene partner really saying to you? Show us how that affects you. Follow that and see where your scene goes.

Director's assist

This is a variation of a Comedysportz game that's done in gibberish. Once the performers become good at it, you can switch to having the two players only speaking in gibberish and the player in the middle is still interpreting the subtext.

How the game is set

Three players sitting in chairs. Put them in a space that would work for a café table. The player in the center is the interpreter.

Number of players

Three

The stage

Three chairs.

How to play

You will need three players, two facing each other with one in the middle facing forward. The person in the middle is going to be the interpreter between the two, they will be interpreting the subtext of what the other is saying.

Player 1 – I like your dress.

Interpreter- He thinks you're very attractive.

Player 2 – This old thing. I just wear it because it is comfortable on a hot day.

Interpreter – You are coming on too strong, she wants you to slow down. Etc. etc.

When we start listening to subtext, we can develop a clearer picture of what's not being said, which will inform us about what is being said. The funny thing about this exercise is that it most benefits the players that are not playing. They get to see the whole picture of how subtext works in scenes. Do this exercise with everyone. Caution them to keep their subtext reading in the PG or lower rating.

Now let's do another exercise.

"What I am hearing is..."

Two players are going to perform a scene. At any time they notice a line that has subtext, they need to respond first with "What I am hearing is..."

For example

Player 1 – I'm not feeling like Thai food today.

Player 2 – But you love Thai food.

Player 1 – Honestly, I am not even hungry.

Player 2 – What I am hearing is that you are not interested in having lunch with me today.

These don't have to be great scenes; we just want people to look deeper into what our partners are really saying.

Some notes to give to help your players

Ask your players to keep it on a PG or lower rating. They are listening with more than their ears. Everything matters. A movement, a way something is said. Say what they feel, not the normal noise we hear in our lives. What's REALLY going on right now?

CONDUCTED STORY

What this game teaches us

Listen and respond ONLY to the last thing that was said. It will teach us to pay attention to the narrative and to be storytellers.

Director's assist

How the game is set

Four to five players form a line downstage center.

Number of players

Four to five players and a conductor.

The stage

Bare stage

How to play

The host or the director kneels in front of the players who are standing shoulder to shoulder on stage to conduct the story. As they point to a player, that player will speak and start telling the story; the conductor will eventually point to someone new and that player will continue the story, picking up from where the previous player left off. This is a great exercise that can also be used in a show. Begin by talking about what makes up a story. The mechanism of the game is that as you point at different players, they are finishing each other's thoughts and sentences.

You can also add a competition element to this. If someone hesitates or messes up, you (or you can even ask the audience) say "You're out of there!" The last person standing finishes the story.

Some notes to give to help your players

We want to create a story. Here's what makes a story.

You have a beginning, a middle, and an end.

You have a hero, a few friends, and a villain maybe?

You can talk to them about the hero's journey (look it up if you don't know it). This is great for the act of listening, but the real challenge is this, can your players continue the story in the voice of the person that was speaking before? Can we listen to what we thought they would say and say that? Now we are working on more than the mechanics of the game. We are trying to work with one mind.

CORE EXERCISE: HOLD UP...

Before we jump into this next exercise, circle up the chairs and let's look at what we call "the beats of a story" these are the actions and the themes we discover in a story. Ask someone in the circle to tell us a story about something that happened to them yesterday. Doesn't have to be funny or super interesting. Just tell us a story for two minutes.

They got up, they ate breakfast, they talked to their dad on the phone about his new RV and how excited he was about camping. Then they met up and went to lunch at a sandwich place they both love.

Once they are done, we are going to see what everyone heard. From the beats of the story, we discover themes. From these themes we can create a new scene. Go around the circle and ask what everyone heard.

- Breakfast
- Father and daughter relationship
- RV lifestyle/RV dealership.
- Sandwich shop.

Those are all of the facts of the story. We can go deeper. Into themes of the story. Ask the circle to think about the bigger picture.

- Starting a new chapter in life
- Eating together brings us closer

- See what toys your parents get excited about

Talk about looking deeper into the story and finding the bigger picture through themes and relationships.

MONOLOGUE INTO A SCENE

What this exercise teaches us

We want to listen to the story and be inspired by it. If someone tells us a story about keeping a house plant alive, we don't want to see that story acted out. Everyone just heard that. Don't tell us what we already know. Instead, the players need to find inspiration from the story and show us something new. Show us a scene that involves themes of rebirth. Show us a scene that deals with loss.

Director's assist

You want your players to take in the story by listening to more than the facts of the story. They need to look for themes, ideas, what are the hopes and dreams they can pull from the story?

How the game is set

One player enters and crosses to center stage. The other two players wait off to the side.

Number of players

3

The stage

Bare stage with chairs available if needed.

How to play

Let's get three people up. One person tells a simple story for a couple of minutes center stage. They will then exit the stage. The two people left are going to do a scene inspired by the story. Caution them that we are not recreating the story. We are improvising a brand NEW scene inspired by the story. Let everyone get a chance to tell a story.

Some notes to give to help your players –

Tell your storytellers to be expressive with their words and feelings. Instead of saying "I had a pastry." tell us details! "I saw a lemon custard in the showcase, it looked golden and flakey and I just knew I had to have it." these details may inspire something in the scene and they can also inform us about the storyteller. This is a person who not only has good taste in their choice of baked confection, they also fall in love at first sight upon seeing it. Give us details about the dad, what does he sound like? What does he do for a living? The story does not have to get longer, but it can be more descriptive.

SCENE INTO A MONOLOGUE

What this game teaches us

Being inspired by elements of a person's or character's story and finding inspiration from that for new scenes.

Director's assist

This is a way to put a button on a scene. A lot of times in improv we only do a story into a scene. But nothing says we can't have a summation at the end of a scene. Plus, it works great later when we start improvising Shakespeare.

Number of players

Three players

The stage

Set up two chairs, they do not need to use them if they do not wish to.

How to play

We did a monologue into a scene; let's flip this idea. Let's get three people up. Ask one to stand off stage ready to tell a story inspired by the scene that just happened. Give the two players a suggestion like "Laundromat" or whatever. Explain to your players that the scene will go on and at some point, the storyteller will edit the scene and tell a true-life story about something that scene reminded them of. So, the scene was maybe about a mom teaching her teenager to fold laundry. The person editing the scene could come out and say something like "I bought one of those plastic boards that help you fold clothing, it's amazing! You just lay your shirt down and flip the different sections of the board and presto! Folded shirt!" Call "scene" and talk to your players about where they could go from that story.

Do this exercise a few more times.

Now, let's join the two exercises. Tell your players someone will tell a story and then you will each do three different stories inspired by that. Then a new storyteller will edit and do a new story inspired by that last scene. The players will be the same characters as before, but their next scenes should be inspired by this new story. Remind them to make big statements at the beginning of the scene. That way everyone can get an idea of where they are going. Then mix up your players and do the exercise once more. Now you have a recipe for a longform format. You could run seven-nine sets of scenes with three stories.

That you do something is far more important than what you do.

-Mick Napier

We improvise to bring our spirits closer to each other. To merge our spirits in the magic of play. And to briefly give birth to universes previously unknown.

-Greg Inda

Improvisational training allows you to refocus the journey when someone loses the path.

-S. Eric Day

OSCAR WINNING MOMENT

What this game teaches us

This game is great for diving into some dramatic improv (which always gets laughs. No, really. It does.)

Director's assist

You're looking for a Poetry Slam moment in the middle of the scene. The same rules apply to the Oscar moment. Be thematic. Be honest in your emotions. Be overly dramatic.

How the game is set

A few chairs.

Number of players

Three players

How to play

This is absolutely one of my favorite games, especially for exploring what's really going on with our characters. And much like poetry slam, it's a game where we can be very thematic. Explain that you are going to have three players do a scene. At any time during that scene when one of the players has a huge line, "And, that's why I will never love again!" You will call out "Oscar winning moment." Now explain that when you watch the Oscars, they show a clip of each person that is nominated for best picture and it's that pivotal moment. That's what they will then do. A short monologue off of the last line they just said. Explain that you want it to build in intensity and emotion, this is Meryl Streep level stuff they need to put out.

Once that ends, they will pick up the scene where it left off. But each player is now more informed and impacted by what just happened. Discuss why hearing that moment has made a huge change in them. That will inspire the next Oscar winning moment.

Each player gets one moment.

Some notes to give to help your players

No one should move or speak as the monologue goes on. They are frozen. Players should make huge statements during the scene. It's your job as the director to pick the right one. This is a great game for a show, but more important is that it's a great game for listening and taking your ideas to level 10.

33

THE SECRETS GAME

What this exercise teaches us

You can always use this as your own little secret in a scene.

Director's assist

This is an insightful exercise that can give the characters on stage a "deal" that only they know. A lot of times I find that players get overwhelmed with the mechanics of a scene or game. This is a wonderful way to occupy that busy space in the brain.

How the game is set

Two players onstage. You will give them a suggestion of a relationship.

Number of players

2

The stage

Put out two chairs cafe style (like they are sitting at a cafe table) with the chairs cheated out a quarter turn.

How to play

This exercise is great for having something in a scene that is just for you. I'll explain: sometimes in a scene, if I don't feel connected to my partner, I'll decide that I have a feeling about them that only I know. Like maybe I have a secret crush. Or maybe I'll decide that they are so cool that I want to be just like them. Just something simple that only I know about. For this we are going to give them something to deal with. Give them a suggestion of a relationship. Like siblings. You are going to whisper in each of their ears a secret that only they know. They cannot say the secret out loud. It's a secret.

You might tell player one "Your butt itches. And the longer the scene goes, the more it itches but no matter what, you cannot scratch it..."

And player two you might say "You want to be a nun. But you can't say that."

Some notes to give to help your players

Explain that if they find themselves in a scene that's not going anywhere, instead of trying to make a change in their scene partner, make a change in themselves and watch how that informs them and everyone else. They can give themselves little ticks that only they know about. And that can help drive character creation.

ENTRANCES AND EXITS

What this game teaches us

We can always leave a scene. But we should have a reason and when we are gone the other players should talk about us.

Here is how the game is set

You really only need a bare stage, but you can put a few chairs on the side for a player to grab if they need it.

Number of players

Four players

How to play

This is a good game to show the value of leaving a scene. I will first explain how to play the short form game. Have the four players line up and then ask the audience for a single word suggestion for each of them.

Example

Player 1 - Hat

Player 2 - Puppy

Player 3 - Crispy

Player 4 - Love

Now, I ask each player to say their word when I point to them. Randomize it so that they all hear each other's words. Then I ask each of them to say everyone else's words. When they can do that you will explain to the audience that each time they hear their own word, they need to enter or exit and have a reason to do so. The fun of this is also the challenge of it. Players can say the other players' words over and over if they want. Sometimes players accidentally say their own word and have to find a reason to exit.

Players' assist

I love this game because one of the lessons it teaches us is that we should be affected by someone leaving or entering a scene. We should always comment on that especially if that comment shows how we feel about the character. This informs the person that just left and when they return, they are a bit different because of it.

It's especially a great way to make multiple person scenes work. Many times when you have more than two players in a scene, it's a bit chaotic. What if someone exits and we're affected by that action? Suddenly, the chaotic multiple person scene has found its heart. For a longform exercise this works well because let's say we have three people on stage and one decides to leave, maybe the next scene is us seeing where that person went. You could do an entire form of three person scenes that always has someone exit and the next scene is exploring where they went and what they did. There is a lot of power in leaving a scene at the right time.

Some notes to give to help your players

Make big statements when you enter or exit a scene. That gives you and everyone else something to go on.

CORE EXERCISE: PLAYING WITH STYLES

Using styles in our performance is an amazing way to play the playwright as we are performing the show. In this section I will show you a method of breaking down a playwright's style in easy to consume bites. The most important thing to remember is that it doesn't need to be perfect. That's impossible. But, if we can hit the beats of a playwright, then we can come pretty close and the audience will think it's magical. Circle up and let's break down one style of movie / television that most everyone knows. The western.

Ask your players to start listing off what kind of people are in a western:

A good guy

A bad guy

A barmaid

A bartender

An old prospector

A farmer and his beautiful unmarried daughter

You get the idea.

Now, let's talk about what everyone wanted in this period of time:

Land of their own.

To make a life in an untamed wilderness.

To strike it rich.

To get married and make a family.

You get the idea. We want to learn what the common man wants That will inform our characters. Now have everyone line up to do some first lines in the style of a western, using the ideas we just came up with. Ask them to try to do all the characters and motivations you discussed. What are their hopes and dreams? Even the bad guys. Bad guys are people too. Someone once said the bad guy is the hero of their own story.

Ok, now let's look at someone like Chekov.

You have people who used to be of a higher class now finding themselves like everyone else after the revolution. You have people who are a bit absurd. Characters that at once seem tragic and funny. Chekov had a habit of calling out what made no sense in his own plays. He had a play within a play that the characters called boring and unwatchable, which is what his own critics would say about his plays.

What did the common people want?

This is post-revolution Russia. The common people suddenly were set on the same level as the aristocracy. It affected both groups in different ways.

Discuss who and what the characters are, what their hopes and dreams were. What was their world like? What did they do for fun?

Then run the first line exercise each time you do it.

Do you need to read all of the plays to do a playwright's style? No. You only need to know the beats of their plays and who the people in them were. After that, it is just improv.

CORE EXERCISE: LET'S DO SOME SHAKESPEARE

I am sure you just read that and said "Wait, what? We can't do Shakespeare! That is really-really hard. Isn't it?"

Nope. In fact, everything we have done in this book has led us to this point. And if you have done everything in this book, in the order I've laid out, you and your players have already learned all the skills you need to do some pretty good Shakespeare. Even if your players have never even seen a Shakespeare play. Let me give you some backstory.

Back in 2005-06, I was teaching a workshop at a high school. I had been working with them for two years and would see the same students as they made their way through school. I was chatting with the teacher and one of the students saw me and said "YES! IMPROV! I LOVE IT! You are hilarious! I loved your class last year!" I asked what he liked best from last year. A game or an exercise that was a favorite? He went blank. He could not remember any of them. When I asked about "yes and..." he had no clue what I was talking about.

After the kid moved on, my teacher friend laughed and said, "Look, your exercises are awesome and the kids have a lot of fun when you are here, but after you are gone their lives go back to their normal levels of absolute chaos. It's just the way it is, they have forgotten everything they have learned about anything. You have no idea how crazy a high schooler's life is. These kids have everything thrown at them all at once and we expect them to survive. So, do not take it personally but the 'yes and..' exercises don't really stick around long at all."

To say I was stunned would be an understatement.

The next thing he said was life-changing for me as a teacher. He said "If you really want to make an impact on these kids, you need to come up with an easy, simple way for them to do something they never expected that they could do. Rethink the way you teach improv, what you want is not a 'lesson' they have to learn, but more of a life experience they get to have. You need to show them how to surprise themselves by what they can do. If you can figure out that, you will make a lasting impact on them, and they will carry that forward. Otherwise, what you are doing is just giving them more lessons and they have too many of those as it is."

Woof. Ok...

I started thinking about ways I could encourage them to take risks and have fun. This is what I came up with. If you can improvise a song or improvise Shakespeare there is nothing you cannot do on an improv stage. Those are the two high-wire acts. Now, I cannot play the piano. But I do know a little bit about Shakespeare.

I started figuring out how I could teach kids to improvise in the style of Shakespeare in just 3 hours. I came up with exercises and games that would show players how to be more dramatic, how to be more empathic, how to speak eloquently, and how to use the top of their intelligence and their emotions to create scenes. This became my teaching method going forward.

And after about a year I had something that worked. And I've been doing it for over a decade now.

What's more, I'm no expert at Shakespeare. I've been an actor since I was 12. I've done more plays than I can list here but have only been in two plays by Shakespeare. Sure, I've read a lot of his works in my life but I'm certainly no expert. What I do know is that his works ring true to all stories we read and watch today. He's the original sitcom writer, the original thriller writer and the original rom com writer. We know all of his stories because we are still retelling them in different forms today.

Let's revisit some of my exercises, but this time you're going to do them with the goal of improvising in the style of Shakespeare. First off, don't tell your players that they will be improvising Shakespeare. Let's keep that between you and me. Start with the Three Line Scenes exercise. We want them to be expressive. Verbose. We want them to say more than they ever would before.

Now let's do the Steal a Line exercise. Tell them not to lose the last exercise. In fact, let them know that you want them to keep using all of these exercises as you build more. Stealing from someone's last line to make your response is a very strong form of "Yes, and..." Because it means you not only listened to the thing your partner just said, you used their line in your response. In a Shakespeare scene, if someone said to me, "Thou are truly a vile and villainous soul!"

I would immediately respond with, "A vile and villainous soul? Me? Nay my lady, for I know mine own heart is true too and ever madly in love with thine own venomous heart that surely beats rapidly in thy chest!" That's not something Shakespeare said, but to an audience, it sounds VERY much like Shakespeare!

Do the Steal a Line exercise and then we want to do the emotional stage. Now, something interesting is going to happen. Even though you haven't told them they will be improvising Shakespeare, once you get to this part, they are going to start speaking in a Shakespearian accent. It almost always happens. Encourage them not to do that. They need to first use their own voice.

After everyone does that, move into poetry slam. Do a set where the suggestion is "love lost," whatever that means to them. Remind them to keep doing the exercises you have already done.

Do it once more, but this time do it with the suggestion of a poem that is "I do they know..." Do the "taking something the wrong way" exercise. Now, let us wrap this up in a merry little bow and tell them we are now going to improvise in the style of Shakespeare!

Explain to them that the only real difference is in what they are doing is talking in an Elizabethan accent. Everything else is the same.

Play an emotional stage. Remind them of these things:

Steal a line.

Say beautiful things.

Take something the wrong way.

Say more words than you think you need to.

You can also take a moment to explain Thou, Thine, Thee

Thou means you and saying "You"

Thine is "Your" it's possessive,

Thee is objective; it places the subject on a pedestal.

After playing Emotional Stage, play Entrances and Exits.

Monologues in a Shakespeare scene

I'm sure everyone is having fun. Let's add some fuel to the fire. Grab your bell and have two players take the stage. Let's play Oscar Winning Moment. This time add the layer that when they hear the bell they need to have their Oscar winning moment be about the other person or their character's hopes and dreams. Let everyone have a chance. Now when that's done, explain that they can take a moment to do a monologue to the audience talking about their real hopes and feelings. That's very much a Shakespearean tool.

Circle everyone up to talk about the people in a Shakespearean play.

The Hero

The Villain

The Lady

The Lover

Twins. There are usually a few sets.

The Merry Jester who is both a villain and a friend.

The King, The Queen, A Baron and even a Duke.

A Ghost!

A Friar or a Priest.

The smart thing that Shakespeare did in his plays is that his characters often introduce themselves and explain their intentions towards the others in the scene. The list goes on and on and all are fun to play.

Now, let's mess with everyone! Have four players take the stage. Tell them you are going to combine Entrances and Exits, Oscar Winning Moment and Emotional stage, ALL AT ONCE!

Remind them of the characters they talked about.

Remind them that scenes are about relationships.

Remind them that today is the day we discover something new. That we uncover a secret. Today is the day that something different happens. Brace yourself...If everything has gone correctly, you are going to see something cool.

You can play any improv game in this style. You could do a whole short form show in the style of Shakespeare. (If you do, I might come see it.) After you have done all of this, gather them around one more time.

Explain this. Playing in the style of Shakespeare is the high bar for improv. If you can improvise in that style? There is nothing you can't do in improv. And all of these skills they have learned translate into good improv.

LONGFORM IMPROV

I've taught at a lot of high schools in my life and the question always comes up "How do we do longform?" and to be honest, I have never had a great answer. Mostly because you can learn an improv game from watching someone else play it. Conversely you can't learn longform by watching someone do it. Longform improv is its own form of theatre and as such it takes a lot of training to do it well. Lucky for us, the ancient gods of improv laid out some tools in shortform that help us teach longform. To get us there I will have to give you an idea of what longform is. (I also have a suggested reading list that includes Charna Halpern and Del Close's book *Truth in Comedy*.)

Longform is, simply put, an improv set that lasts 15 minutes up to 45 minutes from a single suggestion. It can have a set form like what is credited as the first longform called a Harold. Or it can be a loose collection of scenes in what is known as a montage. Here is how I am going to help you teach it: We are going to use short form games to learn longform skills; then, we are going to expand those into longer games; and then we will start doing actual forms. What I want you to remember as a director is this – longform and short form are truly no different. We are just expanding the story past the game. Our characters we create in the first scenes will live on and hopefully return.

This is theatre.

We are storytellers.

We will be improvising a play.

THREE SHORT SCENES

What this exercise teaches us

How to use time dashes in a longform.

Director's assist

We are really only looking to show how we can move a scene along as a longform progresses.

Number of players

Two players.

The stage

Set the stage with two chairs. They do not have to use them but they are there if needed.

How to play

This is a strong longform exercise, and a good character exercise. Here's how it works. Two players will take the stage. Have them sitting side by side with about three feet in between them. They are going to act out three scenes one after the other.

The first scene they are 13 years old.

Then we will do a time dash and in scene two they are 25 years old.

Then a time dash again and they are 75 years old.

As a character exercise, this is a great one because it lets us see our characters change with age. A great teacher of mine, David Razowsky, once said, "Look, the characters we create live on after their scene is over. We need to keep their journey in our minds as the set continues so that if we bring them back or someone calls them back, we know where the character is mentally." A clever note really because it made me think that my characters never truly disappear. They can come back, and they can be changed because of an event we didn't see. Longform improv is like driving a car in reverse through the rearview mirror.

Director's assist

When you want to make the time dash call "FREEZE" rather than "SCENE!" We do this because a FREEZE will pause the players while SCENE means that scene is done. Also explain to your players that each of these scenes is impacted by the ones before. There's a reason we are seeing these moments. HUGE reasons.

Let's see that. Also, the reason I am having them sit is just to keep the players focused on each other. Rather than mindlessly wandering around the stage, we just want them focused on what's happening right now and what it means to us.

FOUR SQUARE

What this game teaches us

This game is a mini longform in a short form matrix.

Director's assist

Longform came out of short form; we can see the tools used in the creation of a longform all through the different short form games.

How the game is set

Four players stand in a square with a bit of room between them.

Number of players

Four players.

The stage

Bare stage

How to play

This is an easy and popular game for shows. It also has all of the mechanics of a longform set. Here's how the game is played. You have four players in a square. Two stand upstage and two stand downstage. The square of players will allow a seamless rotation of four different scenes.

Ask the two people in Scene One (both downstage) to rotate one space to the Right. Now you have one original player and one new player. Keep rotating right until you have cycled through each pair of players and have a total of four scenes. Now have them rotate one more time. You should now have the scene 1 player back in their original spot. If my math is correct...

Give each pair a different suggestion - a location, a relationship, an emotion and something you have always wanted. Explain to them that the players downstage (Scene 1) will start a scene, at any time, you as the director can yell "Right" or "Left" at which time the players will move in that direction in their cube formation; call it whenever you want. You can even have them rotate twice in a row.)

Scene one starts. Let the first scenes establish themselves, then call to rotate. As the scenes go on you want to rotate more and more. It's a lot of fun.

Director's assist

Remind them that scenes are about relationships. Having a funny voice or a big character is great, but if you don't have a point of view and a relationship, they are pretty hollow things. Explain that they don't have to pick up where they left off last. They can jump ahead in time so we see these scenes grow past just now. They can also let the other scenes influence theirs.

Here's how –

They can steal the last line from the scene before. Heck they can steal any line they like and repurpose it as a new line for their scene. If scene one is about building a treehouse, we might find out that another scene is the parents watching the kids build a treehouse from the back door. As a longform exercise this is a perfect example of a longform, especially when the scenes start influencing each other. That's a basic longform in a single exercise.

LE ROUND'

What this game teaches us

This is a very basic longform that is great to help learn how to create narrative over a lot of scenes with different players.

Director's assist

So far, we have been working under the rule of "Respond only to the last thing that was said. Now we want to add in the layer of "Listen and remember ALL of the things that were said..."

How the game is set

Set two chairs on stage and have one player sit. The other players will line up off stage and go in order.

Number of players

Group.

How to play

This is a longform that is great for teaching narrative improv. When I teach this, I put two chairs on stage and have the players line up stage right and a little away from the chairs. Ask the first person in line to sit on the furthest chair stage left.

Explain that you will give them a one-word suggestion to start off. Add that the suggestion can influence the scenes that come after the first one, but it's not a rule. Have the next person in line take the empty chair and explain that these two people will have a short scene, the first person in the stage left chair will eventually find a reason to exit and will go to the back of the line. Tell them that they will ALWAYS be the same characters throughout this exercise. When the player in the stage left seat exits, the remaining player will move over and stay the same character they were in the previous scene.

Let's say it's two characters named Sam and Lynn. Lynn is player one and already on stage, Sam enters, sits down and says a statement based off of the suggestion. They have a short scene with great names and relationships, then player one (Lynn) says "Well! Gotta go make brownies" and exits. Sam moves into the empty seat and Jenny enters. Sam is the same character he was in the last scene, Sam and Jenny have a scene and Sam eventually finds a reason to exit, "I gotta go walk my dog" and it just keeps going. Each character should get two scenes. Once everyone has the idea, pull the chairs back and let people explore the stage in their scenes.

Director's assist

This exercise works best when everyone has a recognizable character. That way when they return, we know who they are. Character work and object work are vital to doing good longform.

ONLY TWO REMAIN II

What this game teaches us

Now we are really going to smash up the La Round and Entrances and Exits

Director's assist

Tell your players that these are short scenes, but this time we are creating a narrative. The scenes should be a continuation of the story like the La Round.

How the game is set

Two people start on stage. Ask for a location that will fit on the stage, let's say a nail salon. Because that's the first suggestion you will get. Everyone thinks about nail salons, but nobody actually goes to them as often as they mean to.

Number of players

Group

The stage

Set two chairs just anywhere. Players can use them or not. Their choice.

How to play

Start with two players. Have everyone line up on one side, the rules are this:

We can only have two people on stage at one time. When someone enters, one person needs to leave.

The person leaving must say why they are leaving.

Someone needs to say something about the person who just left.

This does not need to be sequential but can be. We want to follow the story of the most interesting character or idea.

Players can return, they do not have to think that they are done when they have done it once.

Some notes to give to help your players

Explain to your players that we can always heighten by leaving a scene. Sometimes just the fact that we left can ratchet up everyone else's deal. If you don't feel like you are needed in a scene? Make a huge statement and leave. Let's see what that does.

MONOLOGUE INTO A SCENE II

What this game teaches us

How to look at all the parts of a monologue to create multiple different scenes.

Director's assist

This is just milking more scenes out of a story. We want to see different unrelated scenes.

Number of players

Six players

The stage

Two chairs upstage if needed.

How to play

Now, let's do this exercise again. But let's add a second pair (you will need five people). Someone tells a story. Two people do a scene inspired by that story. At some point, someone from the other pair will do a sweep edit and start a completely new and different scene also by something in the story. Do that a few times. These should be shorter scenes. We just want to explore listening and being inspired by a story.

Now let's add two more. You should now have seven players up. Let's give them each a scene number.

Scene 1

Scene 2

Scene 3

The two people in scene one will do a scene. Then scene two will do a completely new scene inspired by the story. Then scene three will also do a completely new scene inspired by the suggestion. Ok, so once the last scene is ready to edit the director should call freeze! Now, chat with each group and ask where they would take their scene next? What do they feel will be the most interesting thing that could happen to their characters? Have each scene do those things. Then edit and after the third is done, call "Scene!" and get new people up.

This is a Montage. You can keep rotating these scenes for 20 minutes and that's a show you will see anywhere in Chicago, Los Angeles or New York. What we would really like to see is as the montage goes on, these three separate scenes start to merge. Players from scene one start meeting players from scene three. If that happens, you would have a proper longform.

Some notes to give to help your players -

This is a suggestion exercise, we want to see how many different ideas we can get from the monologue and what commonality we find with the other players. Those common things should end up being the scenes created.

CORE EXERCISE: EDITING A SCENE

I've done my best to avoid inter-improv-terms, but editing I will have to explain a bit. Editing is a visual cue that indicates someone is calling SCENE! on your scene. That doesn't make sense at all... Editing is a term we have stolen from film and video editing. A sweep edit is the most common form of an edit. Its name even comes from the film editing term where one scene of a movie is swept aside to reveal the next scene.

(Reads sentence again)

Yeah, I guess that works.

The way we do a sweep edit in improv is at some point in a scene someone will cross the stage along the apron of the stage (usually in a light jaunty jog) thereby "Sweeping" the scene to introduce the next scene. Normally, the person that edits the scene stays on stage for the next one. This is why I like the game Four Square to teach longform. Each time the host calls to rotate left or right, is an edit. The host is building the narrative of the game by dictating the edits. And the players are keeping track of their own scenes while listening to what's going on with the other scenes.

Let's play Four Square again. Get four players up and get a suggestion for all four scenes. Run them through their suggestions by asking them to tell the audience what their scenes are about, just like normal. Now, here's how we are going to change it. This time they will be calling to rotate right or left. But they need to pay attention to the narrative and pick the right spot. Explain to them that they should call to rotate when they feel the scene, they edited has something to come back for.

What do I mean by that? The thing I like about Four Square and any longform is that all four of those scenes are all playing at the same time. We are only focused on the one in front of us, but the other scenes don't just pause waiting for us to return to it, no. They are moving in time as the scene on stage is going. They can travel faster than the scene on stage or slower, but they never stop living. If we pick our edits well, we will be looking for the scene that's up to have a moment. A change has happened and the audience noted it. It's a moment that will change things for those players, enough so that when we return to their scene, we see that something has changed. We edit when we have something to return to.

Now, try to sum that up for your players in three or four short sentences, and please send a copy to me, so I can use it in future versions of this book. I digress. Let these players know that they will have a longer amount of time with this game than the normal three-four minutes. This time they will have 10 minutes. So don't feel rushed. Take your time and explore your relationships and who you are to each other.

Now let's do it again. Set up four new players and give them all the same suggestion. Let's say love, whatever that means to them, and rotate them through it, just like you normally would. Have them say their suggestion even if it sounds stupid. They again will call to rotate right and left.

Now, let's get a new set of four players and run through the rotations, and give them a new suggestion, let's say "being playful," whatever that means to them. But this time they split to the sides of the stage, keeping track of who their partners are. (This is going to fry a few brain cells, but I know they can do it.) They will edit the scenes by calling out Rotate right/left. Remind them this is a game.

Have fun with it. Who cares if something gets messed up? Mistakes are gifts in improv.

Ok, last version – You're going to get some mixture of players up there and ask them to do the same exercise but this time instead of yelling "rotate" they will sweep across the scene to end it, then stay on stage to do the new scene.

Do a jaunty jog downstage right to left to demonstrate and explain that if you see someone doing this during your scene, you've been edited. Go off stage. Now you are doing longform. SO SIMPLE!

Some things to tell your players about edits

You edit the scene when you have something to come back to, like when a huge statement is made or someone has made a huge change in themselves. What we want is to see how that huge thing affected the players. If you are not onstage, you are listening to everything and mentally pocketing all of the facts and names you hear. There's no way to remember them all, but you will be surprised at what the human mind comes up with from a relaxed player who is listening.

If we really want to call a show a longform, we need to at least return to one scene. Otherwise, your longform set was just a collection of scenes. Our imperative in longform is to tell a story that within it has many stories. The bare minimum is one scene coming back later in the show.

Director's assist

The most important takeaway from this exercise is that they understand the mechanics of doing an edit from one scene to the next. They need to work on their listening skills. We don't edit a scene on a laugh, or because we have somehow made the decision that the scene is not working, we edit a scene when the players on stage have somehow changed. Not like, changed into a werewolf or something. They have changed in such a way that their point of view has shifted. That way, we have something to come back to in the next scene. We start the new scene exploring that change and how it has affected the characters. If you direct longform improv with this mind set, our players can relax as the narrative of each scene will write itself, because the players will be honest with each other and have a relationship, they will show us why this day is not like all the rest and their characters will fundamentally be changed people at the end of it. When I am doing any long form, I will make huge declarations in a scene, especially as I feel my fellow players are looking for an edit point. I'll start throwing out lines about what has changed with my character.

CORE EXERCISE: DOING A MONTAGE

A montage is exactly what it sounds like. It's a free form of scenes. Usually there's some type of opening device. Like, a player will get a suggestion of a single word, like "Tacos," then that same player can either tell a true-life story about their own personal experience with tacos or they can come up with a character that has a strong opinion about tacos. When that's done and the player either steps back or is edited by someone who is inspired, the first scene is inspired by that monologue.

Players can always be inspired by the opening. But they can also find inspiration in any scene that's happened. If the suggestion is taco, we could see people waiting in line at a taco stand. The next could be set to show us what's happening inside the taco stand. If we go a little further, we might see one of the people who were waiting for tacos go to their next place. We might see that person then telling a new player how great their date went and all the things they did after tacos. Everything is yours to play with. And you can move forward or even backward in time.

Doing a Montage as a show

This form is an easy form to put up on stage. Typically, the "Get" — which is improv speak for asking for a suggestion — is to get a single word. You can load it up when you ask by trying to get the audience to offer you a word with more meaning to it. Hey everyone! We're going to perform some improv for you, to get us started, by a show of hands, what's a word that is inspired by LOVE?

See how I'm guiding them to give me something they normally wouldn't? I could also say "What's your favorite memory of riding in a car?" A Montage normally lasts about 20-25 minutes. Sometimes, you can play longer, but I would suggest that for a set longer than 25 minutes, you insert another monologue that's either inspired by the original suggestion or the scene right before it.

DIRECTING AN IMPROV SHOW

Casting

When casting a show, I know your first instinct is to go for the players that are the "funniest" but I would also suggest finding the players that are dramatic, who know styles and who just happen to always win at Trivial Pursuit. You really want to build a team that has a little bit of everything. A good improv team has a wide variety of talent. Yes, of course cast the funny ones. But get a few of the dramatic and actor types in the mix as well.

Rehearsal

Any port in a storm will do. And that is the great thing about an improv show. It's easy to move to a lot of places. The only thing I've never had a lot of success with is rehearsing in someone's home. There are just too many distractions for the cast to focus. There's a dog, there's a cat, there's both. Is that a baby goat??? Or the TV is on in another part of the house. Find a place that does not have those distractions. That being said, rehearsal is wherever you all meet up. I would also advocate that you set a time and stick to it. If you rehearse Mondays at 6pm, then live up to that. Start on time and end on time.

Noting a show

I do not actually write a lot of notes during a show. Typically, I write who was in each scene and what the scene was about and the suggestion if it's a short form show. I will also add little memories like "Relationship!" or "Why did we need the snake?" Then after a show I will go through each scene. If the scene was good? That's all we need to say. Did the scene need something? We want to say that. Overall, we want to give notes that will help the players move forward on their journey. If you think of a note that isn't going to do that, skip that note. It's not constructive. Especially since the show you just did will never be repeated.

Dressing for a show

Putting up a show is a big deal. And when the lights go up, you want to look ready to put on a show. Now, some teams have the money to do a run of T-Shirts that say "IMPROVER BEHAVIOR!" and wear matching headbands. But not everyone can afford that.

My advice is this

The team should at least be dressed in the same manner. Tennis shoes, blue jeans and black t-shirts are fine. You could change the t-shirts to dress shirts and add a tie, that's fine. Everyone could be wearing 1990s tracksuits! As long as everyone is dressed within that same category. A great rule is you should try to dress nicer than your audience.

I would also avoid these

T-shirts with logos. Or ones that say something. Especially if it is humorous. Never give your T-shirt the opportunity to be funnier than you.

Pick safe shoes that grip the stage.

No hats, no sunglasses, no capes. Yes, you read that right. I once had to tell a player that they could not wear a blue superhero cape in a show. Now, if they all had one, I would have let it go because, at least they looked like a team. But this was just one player and their cape. Every scene would have a superhero.

This should go without saying, but everyone should be showered and have a nice smell about them.

TIPS FOR BEING A GOOD SHOW HOST

First and foremost, always keep in mind that you want people to feel comfortable at the show. It's your task as the host to provide that safe wonderful space. I like to think that I'm hosting a party of 126 people in my living room. I check in with them and try to have a conversational tone.

Start off by thanking the audience for coming to the show. Especially if it's on a Tuesday night. At 9:30.

Welcome them to the theater and tell them the name of the show. Explain how the show will work. Let them know any rules about the show like No Flash Photography. Hey, don't talk during the show. Whatever.

Introduce the players and have them form a backline and introduce themselves.

Start the show with explaining the first game and how you want to handle audience suggestions. Like "We would like our audience to raise a hand for a suggestion." Whatever works, but you should lay it out. From here, you can continue hosting, or the better option is to have the players introduce their own games and ask for a suggestion.

Ideally this would sound like "My two friends and I are going to play a game for you called 'Sit, Stand, Lean.' To get us started, by a show of hands, what's a location that would fit on this stage?"

When the show is over the host comes out, thanks the audience for enjoying the show (hopefully) and thanks any crew, light people, sound or music folks. Then ask the players to say their name one more time. Then say your name and exit.

Some things I would avoid

If you're the host, please don't demand that the audience give more applause. That's great for a basketball game, but this is theatre. No one runs out and says "Come on folks! Give it up for HAROLD PINTER! WOOT!" Plus, most times when I see that, the person asking us to applaud more has not done anything that would warrant that action. Being cool and conversational will go a long way.

Dress nice. The host should always look as nice or nicer than the players. If the players are in suits, at least try to match. Avoid loud shirts or shabby clothing.

Closing a show

Your last game just ended. The lights went down and hopefully some fun upbeat music starts playing. Lights up and you, the host of the night, take the stage! Be gracious, thank everyone for coming. Now bring the cast back out to form a backline behind you. Tell them the name of the show and have the cast say their names one more time. Now we need to thank the people who were not on stage. Thank the stage manager, the lights and sound people, if you have an accompanist thank them. Lastly, thank the audience one last time and then have everyone on stage do a final bow and exit.

It's a nice touch to have the cast meet and greet after a show. Once that's done, have the cast meet for notes.

Noting a show

I do not actually write a lot of notes during a show. Typically, I write who was in each scene and what the scene was about and the suggestion if it's a short form show. I will also add little memories like "Relationship!" or "Why did we need the snake?" Then after a show I will go through each scene. If the scene was good? That's all we need to say. Did the scene need something? We want to say that. Overall, we want to give notes that will help the players move forward on their journey. If you think of a note that isn't going to do that, skip that note. It's not constructive. Especially since the show you just did will never be repeated.

READING LIST

Over the years teachers I've worked with have asked me what books they might read to help them teach improv. The title of my own book is drawn from that question. It's not an easy task to learn an art form that is tied so deeply to being in the moment. When I'm teaching, I want everyone to be up and ready to play. That's the best way to learn about improv hands down.

But the life of a teacher is not made up of an abundance of free time. And if you need to teach your students improv, reading is often the only way you can get the education you need. These books should be on your "Must Read" list:

Improvisation For the Theater by Viola Spolin

Improvise: Scene from the inside out by Mick Napier

A Subversives Guide to Improvisation: Moving Beyond "Yes, And" by David Razowsky

Jill Benard's Small Cute Book of Improv by Jill Benard

The most important thing when reading about improvisation is to make an actionable list. When you read something that makes you think "I need to remember that next time we do improv!" stop what you're doing and add it to your list, be it on your phone or on paper.

But don't depend on your memory to do that work for you. Because you and I both know that's not going to work. Make your list. Never stop adding to it.

ABOUT THE AUTHOR

Alan Hawkins, a seasoned improviser with experience in both Los Angeles and Chicago, has been captivating audiences and nurturing new talent since 2004. He wears many hats - performer, director, and teacher - having honed his craft at prestigious institutions like The Second City Conservatory and iO West.

Beyond the stage, Alan has graced festivals across the US with his improv group, Extra Shelves, and even shared his expertise internationally. He currently calls Seattle home, where he's a ensemble member of Unexpected Productions, the longest-running Theatersports theater in America.

When not on stage, Alan enjoys life in the Pacific Northwest with his wife, their two very creative children, and their beloved Corgi.

Made in United States
Troutdale, OR
03/20/2024